Informing the legislative debate since 1914

Shutdown of the Federal Government:
Causes, Processes, and Effects

Clinton T. Brass, Coordinator
Specialist in Government Organization and Management

September 8, 2014

Congressional Research Service

7-5700

www.crs.gov

RL34680

Summary

When federal agencies and programs lack funding after the expiration of full-year or interim appropriations, the agencies and programs experience a funding gap. If funding does not resume in time to continue government operations, then, under the Antideficiency Act, an agency must cease operations, except in certain situations when law authorizes continued activity. The criteria that flow from the Antideficiency Act for determining which activities are affected are complex.

Failure of the President and Congress to reach agreement on full-year or interim funding measures occasionally has caused shutdowns of affected federal government activities. The longest such shutdown lasted 21 full days during FY1996, from December 16, 1995, to January 6, 1996. More recently, a funding gap commenced on October 1, 2013, the first day of FY2014, after funding for the previous fiscal year expired. Because funding did not resume on October 1, affected agencies began to cease operations and furlough personnel that day. A 16-full-day shutdown ensued, the first to occur in over 17 years.

Government shutdowns have necessitated furloughs of several hundred thousand federal employees, required cessation or reduction of many government activities, and affected numerous sectors of the economy. This report discusses

- *causes* of shutdowns, including the legal framework under which they may occur;

- *processes* related to how agencies may plan for the contingency of a shutdown;

- *effects* of shutdowns, focusing especially on federal personnel and government operations; and

- *issues* related to shutdowns that may be of interest to Congress.

This CRS report is intended to address questions that arise frequently related to the topic of government shutdowns. However, the report does not closely track developments related to the appropriations process for a given fiscal year. For links to CRS resources related to annual appropriations, see the "CRS Appropriations Status Table," at http://crs.gov/pages/AppropriationsStatusTable.aspx.

Additional resources related to funding gaps and shutdowns are identified below.

Agency Shutdown Plans

For links to agency shutdown plans (also sometimes called "contingency plans") of varying dates, see the Office of Management and Budget's (OMB's) website, at http://www.whitehouse.gov/omb/contingency-plans.

CRS Written Products

- ***Listing of CRS written products related to FY2014 shutdown.*** For an annotated list of CRS products that relate to the FY2014 funding gap, shutdown, and related status of appropriations, see CRS Report R43250, *CRS Resources on the FY2014 Funding Gap, Shutdown, and Status of Appropriations*, by Justin Murray.

- ***Funding gaps history.*** For discussion of funding gaps in recent decades and a more detailed chronology of legislative actions and funding gaps that led to the two shutdowns of FY1996 and the shutdown of FY2014, see CRS Report RS20348, *Federal Funding Gaps: A Brief Overview*, by Jessica Tollestrup.

- ***Past government shutdowns.*** For an annotated list of historical documents and other resources related to past government shutdowns, see CRS Report R41759, *Past Government Shutdowns: Key Resources*, by Jared C. Nagel and Justin Murray.

CRS Services

For questions concerning the impact of a shutdown on a specific agency or program in the executive branch, legislative branch operations, or judicial branch operations,

- see the contact information for CRS subject matter experts who are listed in CRS Report R41723, *Funding Gaps and Government Shutdowns: CRS Experts*;

- use the "place a request" function on the CRS website;

- call CRS at 7-5700; or

- see the "Key Policy Staff" table at the end of this report.

Contents

Contacts

Budget Negotiations and Choices

It has been said that "conflict is endemic to budgeting."[1] If conflict within Congress or between Congress and the President impedes the timely enactment of annual appropriations acts or continuing resolutions, a government shutdown may occur. Along these lines, several options may present themselves to Congress and the President during high-stakes negotiations over appropriations measures. The options include

- coming to agreement on regular appropriations acts by October 1, the beginning of a new fiscal year;

- using one or more interim continuing resolutions (CRs) to extend temporary funding beyond the beginning of a fiscal year, until a point in time when negotiators make final decisions about full-year funding levels; or

- not agreeing on full-year or interim appropriations acts, resulting in a temporary funding gap and a corresponding shutdown of affected federal government activities.

If Congress and the President pursue the second or third options, they may agree on full-year appropriations after the beginning of the fiscal year. These agreements may provide funding through regular appropriations acts, singly or in omnibus legislation, or less commonly, through a full-year CR. Congress and the President frequently agree on full-year or interim funding without coming to an impasse.[2] On other occasions, however, Congress and the President may not come to an accommodation in time to prevent a temporary funding gap. If a funding gap begins and funding does not appear likely to resume during the first calendar day of the gap, the federal government generally begins a "shutdown" of affected activities. The criteria for determining which activities are affected are complex, as discussed later in this report.

This report discusses the causes of funding gaps and shutdowns of the federal government, processes that are associated with shutdowns, and how agency operations may be affected by shutdowns.[3] The report concludes with a discussion of potential issues for Congress.

---

[1] Irene S. Rubin, "Understanding the Role of Conflict in Budgeting," in Roy T. Meyers, ed., *Handbook of Government Budgeting* (San Francisco, CA: Jossey-Bass, 1999), p. 30.

[2] For discussion of the potential functions and impacts of CRs, see CRS Report R42647, *Continuing Resolutions: Overview of Components and Recent Practices*, by Jessica Tollestrup; and CRS Report RL34700, *Interim Continuing Resolutions (CRs): Potential Impacts on Agency Operations*, by Clinton T. Brass.

[3] This report focuses on funding gaps and shutdowns that are associated with annual appropriations acts. It does not focus on shutdowns that may occur when a specific program or agency is funded by legislation other than annual appropriations acts, and the statutory authorization for the program or agency expires. Nevertheless, these "expired authorization" shutdowns are similar in many ways to broader "annual appropriations" shutdowns. An example of an expired authorization shutdown occurred in early 2010, when authorization for certain surface transportation programs and trust funds expired after 11:59 p m. on February 28, 2010. The expiration caused a lapse in authority to expend funds that, among other things, affected certain construction projects on federal lands and required nearly 2,000 U.S. Department of Transportation employees to be furloughed. On March 2, 2010, P.L. 111-144 reauthorized these activities (124 Stat. 45). On April 15, 2010, P.L. 111-157 provided compensation to furloughed federal employees and ratified retroactively all "essential actions" taken during the lapse by federal employees, contractors, and grantees to "protect life and property and to bring about orderly termination of Government functions" (124 Stat. 1118).

Causes of Federal Shutdowns

The federal fiscal year begins on October 1. For agencies and programs that rely on discretionary funding through annual appropriations acts, Congress and the President must enact interim or full-year appropriations by this date if many governmental activities are to continue operating.[6] If interim or full-year appropriations are not enacted into law, the interval in which agency appropriations are not enacted is called a "funding gap."[7] In addition, a funding gap may occur if a CR's interim funding expires and another CR or regular appropriations bill is not enacted immediately thereafter. When a funding gap begins and appears likely to continue a full calendar day or longer, the federal government

> **Box 1. Are a Funding Gap and a Shutdown the Same Thing?**
>
> No; although a shutdown may result from a funding gap, the two events are distinct. This is because a funding gap may result in a shutdown of affected projects or activities in some instances but not others. For example, if a funding gap is of a short duration, or if a funding gap occurs over a weekend, agencies may not have enough time to complete a shutdown of affected projects and activities before funding resumes.[4] Consequently, what counts as a shutdown may, to some extent, be difficult to document. In addition, the Office of Management and Budget has previously indicated that a shutdown of agency operations during the first full calendar day of a funding gap may be postponed or avoided if it appears that a CR or regular appropriations bill is likely to be enacted later during that same day.[5]

generally begins a "shutdown" of the affected activities (see **Box 1**). In general, a shutdown implies the furlough of certain personnel and curtailment of agency activities and services. There are multiple exceptions to this general process, however, as this report explains later. Programs that are funded by laws other than annual appropriations acts—such as entitlements like Social Security and other mandatory spending—also may be affected by a funding gap, if program execution relies on activities that receive annually appropriated funding.

---

[4] For example, *Congressional Quarterly* reported in one case that "[t]hree days after several government departments ran out of money [on Friday, November 11, 1983, during FY1984], President Reagan [on] Nov. 14 signed a stopgap spending bill to fund those agencies through the Sept. 30, 1984, end of the fiscal year. Because of a three-day, Veterans Day holiday weekend and White House assurances that Reagan would sign the bill (H.J.Res. 413—P.L. 98-151), there was no disruption in government services." See *Congressional Quarterly Almanac, 1983*, vol. XXXIX (Washington, DC: Congressional Quarterly, 1984), p. 528.

[5] The Office of Management and Budget effectively has taken the view that if funding authority expires at the end of a day (e.g., Friday, April 8, 2011), but continuing or full-year authority is enacted at any time during the next calendar day (e.g., Saturday, April 9, 2011), where enacted means signed by the President after passing both chambers of Congress, no funding gap or shutdown occurs. For example, in the case of a near-shutdown when funding expired the night of April 8, 2011, OMB directed agencies to continue operating normally in anticipation that Congress would pass and the President would sign legislation the next day to resume funding. See U.S. Executive Office of the President, Office of Management and Budget (hereinafter OMB), Memorandum M-11-13, *Planning for Agency Operations During a Lapse in Government Funding*, April 7, 2011, p. 3, and OMB Memorandum M-11-14, *Anticipated Enactment of a Continuing Resolution*, April 8, 2011, p. 1, at http://www.whitehouse.gov/omb/memoranda_default/.

[6] Discretionary funding refers to budget authority (i.e., authority to incur financial obligations that result in government expenditures) that is provided in and controlled by annual appropriations acts. By contrast, mandatory funding refers to budget authority that is provided in and controlled by laws other than annual appropriations acts. Some budget authority provided in annual appropriations acts for certain programs is treated as mandatory, however, because the relevant authorizing legislation entitles beneficiaries to receive payment or otherwise obligates the government to make payment. See U.S. Government Accountability Office (formerly General Accounting Office; hereinafter GAO), *A Glossary of Terms Used in the Federal Budget Process*, GAO-05-734SP, September 2005, pp. 46, 66; and CRS Report RS20129, *Entitlements and Appropriated Entitlements in the Federal Budget Process*, by Bill Heniff Jr.

[7] For discussion, see CRS Report RS20348, *Federal Funding Gaps: A Brief Overview*, by Jessica Tollestrup. Some observers use the alternative terms "lapse in appropriations" or "appropriations hiatus" instead of "funding gap."

Experience from FY1977 to Present

Funding gaps and government shutdowns have occurred in the past when Congress and the President did not enact regular appropriations bills by the beginning of the fiscal year.[8] They also have occurred when Congress and the President did not come to an agreement on stop-gap funding through a CR. As noted in another CRS report, six relatively lengthy funding gaps occurred from FY1977 to FY1980, ranging from 8 to 17 full days.[9] These funding gaps occurred before the Department of Justice issued legal opinions in 1980 and 1981 about agency activities that may continue during a funding gap. The opinions, which are discussed later in this report, were more restrictive in their implications about allowable activities during a funding gap compared to what agencies had done in the past. After FY1980, funding gaps continued to occur at times, but the durations of funding gaps shortened considerably compared to prior years. From FY1981 to FY1995, nine funding gaps occurred with durations of up to three full days.

A significant exception to the trend toward shorter funding gaps occurred in FY1996. Two funding gaps and corresponding shutdowns of affected activities ensued, amounting to five full days during November 1995 and 21 full days during December 1995-January 1996.[10] In the wake of the FY1996 experience, funding gaps did not occur again for over 17 years. Nevertheless, another relatively long funding gap began on October 1, 2013, the first day of FY2014, after funding for FY2013 expired at the end of September.[11] A 16-full-day shutdown of affected activities followed.

Legal Framework for How Shutdowns Have Occurred

The Constitution, statutory provisions, court opinions, and Department of Justice (DOJ) opinions provide the legal framework for how funding gaps and shutdowns have occurred in recent decades.[12] Article I, Section 9 of the Constitution states that "No Money shall be drawn from the Treasury, but in Consequence of Appropriations made by Law." Federal employees and contractors cannot be paid, for example, if appropriations in the first place have not been enacted. Nevertheless, it would appear to be possible under the Constitution for the government to make contracts or other obligations even if it lacks funds to pay for these commitments.[13] Several

---

[8] For an annotated list of official documents and other resources related to past government shutdowns, see CRS Report R41759, *Past Government Shutdowns: Key Resources*, by Jared C. Nagel and Justin Murray.

[9] CRS Report RS20348, *Federal Funding Gaps: A Brief Overview*, by Jessica Tollestrup. FY1977 marked the first full fiscal year of implementing the congressional budget process established by the Congressional Budget Act of 1974.

[10] President William J. Clinton and the 104th Congress were engaged in extended negotiations over budget policy. For a detailed chronology and graphical depiction of the FY1996 appropriations process, including the two funding gaps, see CRS Report RS20348, *Federal Funding Gaps: A Brief Overview*, by Jessica Tollestrup.

[11] This occurred during the 113th Congress in the wake of deliberations among the House, the Senate, and President Barack Obama regarding the status of the Patient Protection and Affordable Care Act (ACA). For discussion, see CRS Report R43246, *Affordable Care Act (ACA) and the Appropriations Process: FAQs Regarding Potential Legislative Changes and Effects of a Government Shutdown*, coordinated by C. Stephen Redhead.

[12] The DOJ opinions were written to guide actions in the executive branch. The legislative and judicial branches are not guided officially by executive branch documents regarding the Antideficiency Act. However, the two branches continue to be guided by the Constitution and the act itself, and may look to executive branch guidelines as a point of reference. For legal analysis of funding gaps, see GAO, *Principles of Federal Appropriations Law*, 3rd ed., vol. II, GAO-06-382SP, February 2006, chapter 6, pp. 6-146 - 6-159.

[13] For discussion, see prepared statement of Walter Dellinger, Assistant Attorney General, in U.S. Congress, Senate Committee on the Budget and House Committee on the Budget, *Effects of Potential Government Shutdown*, hearing, (continued...)

provisions of law—which commonly are referred to as the Antideficiency Act—generally prevent this from happening, however. The act, which evolved over time and is located in Title 31 of the *U.S. Code*, prohibits federal officials from obligating funds before an appropriations measure has been enacted, except as authorized by law.[14] The act also prohibits acceptance of voluntary services and employment of personal services exceeding what has been authorized by law.[15] Therefore, the Antideficiency Act generally prohibits agencies from continued operation in the absence of appropriations. Failure to comply with the act may result in criminal sanctions, fines, and removal. The act makes exceptions to the prohibitions on acceptance of voluntary services and employment of personal services, however, for "emergencies involving the safety of human life or the protection of property."[16]

For years leading up to 1980, many federal agencies continued to operate during a funding gap, "minimizing all nonessential operations and obligations, believing that Congress did not intend that agencies close down," while waiting for the enactment of annual appropriations acts or CRs.[17] In 1980 and 1981, however, then-U.S. Attorney General Benjamin R. Civiletti issued two opinions that more strictly interpreted the Antideficiency Act, along with the law's exceptions, in the context of a funding gap.[18]

The Attorney General's opinions addressed "the scope of currently existing legal and constitutional authorities for the continuance of government functions during a temporary lapse in appropriations."[19] In brief, the opinions stated that, with some exceptions, the head of an agency could avoid violating the Antideficiency Act only by suspending the agency's operations until the enactment of an appropriation. In the absence of appropriations, exceptions would be allowed only when there is "some reasonable and articulable connection between the function to be performed and the safety of human life or the protection of property."[20] In addition, "there must be some reasonable likelihood that the safety of human life or the protection of property would be compromised, in some degree, by delay in the performance of the function in question."[21] Apart from this broad category of "human life and property" exceptions to the act, the Civiletti opinions

---

(...continued)

104th Cong., 1st sess., September 19, 1995, S.Hrg. 104-175 (Washington, DC: GPO, 1995), p. 18. Some commentators, however, have expressed a contrary view. See Jim Schweiter and Herb Fenster, *Government Contract Funding under Continuing Resolutions*, 95 Fed. Cont. Rep. 180, note 17 (February 15, 2011).

[14] 31 U.S.C. §1341. The Antideficiency Act (31 U.S.C. §§1341-1342, §§1511-1519) is discussed in CRS Report RL30795, *General Management Laws: A Compendium*, by Clinton T. Brass et al., pp. 93-97. GAO provides information on the act, at http://www.gao.gov/legal/lawresources/antideficiencybackground.html.

[15] 31 U.S.C. §1342.

[16] Ibid.

[17] GAO, *Funding Gaps Jeopardize Federal Government Operations*, PAD-81-31, March 3, 1981, pp. i, 2.

[18] 43 Op. Att'y Gen. 224 (April 25, 1980) (hereinafter, "1980 Civiletti opinion"), 43 Op. Att'y Gen. 293 (January 16, 1981) (hereinafter, "1981 Civiletti opinion"). The Civiletti opinions are available in electronic form in the appendices of a GAO report. See GAO, *Funding Gaps Jeopardize Federal Government Operations*, PAD-81-31, March 3, 1981, Appendices IV (1980 Civiletti opinion) and VIII (1981 Civiletti opinion), at http://www.gao.gov/assets/140/132616.pdf. For a detailed discussion of the history of, and exceptions to, the Antideficiency Act, see GAO, *Principles of Federal Appropriations Law*, 3rd ed., vol. II, pp. 6-146 - 6-159.

[19] 1981 Civiletti opinion, in GAO, *Funding Gaps Jeopardize Federal Government Operations*, PAD-81-31, March 3, 1981, Appendix VIII, p. 76.

[20] Ibid., p. 86.

[21] Ibid.

---

identified another category: those exceptions that are "authorized by law." GAO later summarized the 1981 Civiletti opinion as identifying four sub-types of "authorized by law" exceptions:[22]

- Activities funded with appropriations of budget authority that do not expire at the end of one fiscal year, such as multiple-year and no-year appropriations.[23] These activities may continue when the multiple-year and no-year appropriations still have budget authority that is available for obligation at the time of a funding gap. In addition, agencies that receive most or all of their budget authority for their day-to-day operations through means that are not dependent on annual appropriations acts, such as the U.S. Postal Service, would fall under this exception.

- Activities authorized by statutes that expressly permit obligations in advance of appropriations, such as contract authority.[24]

- Activities "authorized by necessary implication from the specific terms of duties that have been imposed on, or of authorities that have been invested in, the agency." The Civiletti opinion illustrated this abstract concept by citing the situation when benefit payments under an entitlement program are funded from other-than-one-year appropriations (i.e., where benefit payments are not subject to a funding gap, because they are authorized by permanent entitlement authority),[25] but the salaries of personnel who administer the program are funded by one-year appropriations (i.e., the salaries are subject to a funding gap). In this situation, the Attorney General offered the view that continued availability of money for benefit payments would necessarily imply that continued administration of the program is authorized by law at some level and therefore excepted from the Antideficiency Act.[26]

- Obligations "necessarily incident to presidential initiatives undertaken within his constitutional powers," such as the power to grant pardons and reprieves. GAO later expressed the view that this same rationale would apply to legislative branch agencies that incur obligations "necessary to assist the Congress in the performance of its constitutional duties."[27]

For its part, the 1980 Civiletti opinion included in the "authorized by law" exception an inference that federal officers may, in the temporary absence of appropriations, exercise authority to incur

---

[22] Portions of this text draw from GAO, *Principles of Federal Appropriations Law*, 3rd ed., vol. II, pp. 6-149 - 6-150. GAO also noted that the courts have added to the list of exceptions to the Antideficiency Act (ibid., p. 6-152).

[23] The term "multiple-year budget authority" refers to budget authority that remains available for obligation for a fixed period of time in excess of one fiscal year. The term "no-year budget authority" refers to budget authority that remains available for an indefinite period of time (e.g., "to remain available until expended"). See GAO, *A Glossary of Terms Used in the Federal Budget Process*, GAO-05-734SP, September 2005, p. 22.

[24] For an explanation of contract authority, see ibid., p. 21.

[25] In this case, budget authority is available to make payments as a result of previously enacted legislation and is available without further legislation. "Entitlement authority" refers to authority to make payments (including loans and grants) for which budget authority is not provided in advance by appropriations acts to any person or government if, under the provisions of the law containing such authority, the federal government is legally required to make the payments to persons or governments that meet the requirements established by law. See ibid., pp. 22-23 and 47.

[26] See the section of this report titled "Effects on Mandatory Spending Programs" for a more detailed discussion.

[27] GAO, *Principles of Federal Appropriations Law*, 3rd ed., vol. II, p. 6-150.

minimal obligations necessary to closing their agencies in an orderly way.[28] Subsequently, the Office of Management and Budget (OMB) interpreted this exception to fall under the "necessary implication" sub-type of the "authorized by law" exception.[29]

In 1990, in response to the 1981 Civiletti opinion, Congress amended 31 U.S.C. §1342 to clarify that "the term 'emergencies involving the safety of human life or the protection of property' does not include ongoing, regular functions of government the suspension of which would not imminently threaten the safety of human life or the protection of property."[30] DOJ's Office of Legal Counsel (OLC) issued a memorandum in 1995 that interpreted the effect of the amendment (hereinafter "1995 OLC opinion").[31] The 1995 OLC opinion said one aspect of the 1981 Civiletti opinion's description of emergency governmental functions should be modified in light of the amendment (suggesting that the phrase "in some degree" be replaced with "in some significant degree"),[32] but that the 1981 opinion otherwise "continues to be a sound analysis of the legal authorities respecting government operations" during a funding gap.[33] More recently, OMB summarized its interpretation of exceptions to the Antideficiency Act in several memoranda. The memoranda were issued to agencies in April and December 2011 (regarding FY2011 and FY2012 annual appropriations, respectively), and September 2013 (regarding FY2014 annual appropriations).[34]

Notably, the opinions of OLC and OMB do not permit outlays—such as the issuance of checks, disbursement of cash, or electronic transfer of funds—to liquidate federal obligations for operations that lack appropriated funding during a shutdown. Rather, OLC and OMB have interpreted the Antideficiency Act as including exceptions that provide only the authority to incur obligations that will be paid upon enactment of appropriations in the future.

Observers sometimes wish to contrast the effect of a government shutdown, on one hand, with the effect of the federal government reaching its statutory debt limit and not raising it, on the other. The two situations are distinct in terms of their effects on agency operations and on federal government payments to liquidate obligations (see **Box 2**).

---

[28] 1980 Civiletti opinion, in GAO, *Funding Gaps Jeopardize Federal Government Operations*, PAD-81-31, March 3, 1981, Appendix IV, p. 67.

[29] See, for example, OMB Memorandum M-11-13, *Planning for Agency Operations During a Lapse in Government Funding*, April 7, 2011, pp. 5-6.

[30] GAO, *Principles of Federal Appropriations Law*, 3rd ed., vol. II, p. 6-151, citing provisions in P.L. 101-508, 104 Stat. 1388, at 1388-621, that currently are codified at 31 U.S.C. §1342.

[31] U.S. Department of Justice, Office of Legal Counsel, *Government Operations in the Event of a Lapse in Appropriations*, memorandum from Walter Dellinger, Assistant Attorney General, for Alice Rivlin, Director, Office of Management and Budget, August 16, 1995, reprinted in U.S. Congress, Senate Committee on the Budget and House Committee on the Budget, *Effects of Potential Government Shutdown*, hearing, 104th Cong., 1st sess., September 19, 1995, S.Hrg. 104-175 (Washington, DC: GPO, 1995), pp. 77-85. The 1995 OLC opinion also may be found in electronic form, at http://www.justice.gov/olc/appropriations2 htm.

[32] That is, in light of the intervening amendments, the 1995 OLC opinion required the safety of human life or the protection of property to be compromised "in some significant degree" for a function to be considered excepted. The opinion concluded that "the emergencies exception applies only to cases of threat to human life or property where the threat can be reasonably said to [be] near at hand and demanding of immediate response." Ibid.

[33] Ibid., p. 78.

[34] OMB Memorandum M-11-13, *Planning for Agency Operations During a Lapse in Government Funding*, April 7, 2011, pp. 4-6; OMB Memorandum M-12-03, *Planning for Agency Operations During a Lapse in Government Funding*, December 15, 2011, Attachment 1 (first three pages of non-paginated attachment); and OMB Memorandum M-13-22, *Planning for Agency Operations During a Potential Lapse in Appropriations*, September 17, 2013, pp. 3-5.

Box 2. Distinction Between a Government Shutdown and a Debt Limit Impasse

In a shutdown situation, Congress and the President have not enacted interim or full-year appropriations for an agency for part or all of a fiscal year. An expectation exists, however, that these appropriations will be enacted in the future. In this case, the agency temporarily does not have budget authority available for obligation for things like salaries, rent, or grants to states. Under the Antideficiency Act, the agency may obligate some funds in certain "excepted" areas, but these obligations are highly restricted. As a consequence, the agency must shut down non-excepted activities, and the federal government may not make actual payment (i.e., outlays) for excepted or non-excepted activities until budget authority is provided, or unless another source of budget authority is utilized.

In a debt limit impasse, by contrast, the government no longer has an ability to borrow to finance its obligations.[35] In such a situation, an agency may continue to obligate any available budget authority that has previously been enacted. However, the Treasury Department may not be able to liquidate all obligations that are due to be paid, because of a shortage of cash. As a result, the federal government would need to rely solely on incoming revenues to finance obligations. If this occurs during a period when the federal government is running a deficit, the dollar amount of newly incurred federal obligations would exceed the dollar amount of newly incoming revenues. This may result in delays in federal payments and disruptions in government operations.

OMB and Agency Processes for Shutdown Planning

Annual Instructions for Agencies

In the annually revised *Circular No. A-11*, OMB provides instructions to executive branch agencies on how to prepare for and operate during a funding gap.[36] The circular cites the two Civiletti opinions and the 1995 OLC opinion as background and guidance. The circular also establishes two "policies" regarding the absence of appropriations:

- a prohibition on incurring obligations unless the obligations are otherwise authorized by law and

- permission to incur obligations "as necessary for orderly termination of an agency's functions," but prohibition of any disbursement (i.e., payment).

The circular also directs agency heads to develop and maintain shutdown plans. These plans sometimes also have been called "contingency plans."

Prior to the 2011 revision of *Circular No. A-11*, the circular broadly indicated that the plans were to be submitted to OMB when initially prepared and also when revised. The plans themselves were required to contain summary information about the number of employees expected to be on-board before a shutdown and also the number of employees who would be "retained" (i.e., excepted from furlough) during a shutdown. With the August 2011 revision of the circular, however, OMB newly required that these plans contain more detailed information, be updated under certain conditions, and be updated periodically, with a minimum frequency of a four-year schedule starting August 1, 2014. OMB's change in instructions occurred four months after Congress and the President almost came to an impasse, in April 2011, on FY2011 appropriations.

---

[35] For further discussion of the federal debt limit, see CRS Report R41633, *Reaching the Debt Limit: Background and Potential Effects on Government Operations*, coordinated by Mindy R. Levit.

[36] OMB, *Circular No. A-11: Preparation, Submission, and Execution of the Budget*, July 2014, Section 124, at http://www.whitehouse.gov/omb/circulars_a11_current_year_a11_toc. For information about OMB, see CRS Report RS21665, *Office of Management and Budget (OMB): A Brief Overview*, by Clinton T. Brass.

After the FY2014 shutdown, OMB's 2014 revision to the circular changed the schedule for updates to shutdown plans. Henceforward, agencies were instructed to submit updated plans to OMB for review with a minimum frequency of every two years, beginning August 1, 2015.

Under OMB's current instructions from *Circular No. A-11*, agency heads are told to use the DOJ opinions and the circular, in consultation with the agencies' general counsels, to "decide what agency activities are excepted or otherwise legally authorized to continue during a lapse in appropriations."[37] Furthermore, these plans are required to address agency actions in two distinct time windows of a shutdown: an initial period of one to five days, which OMB characterized as a "short" lapse, and a second period if a shutdown were to extend further. Among other things, a shutdown plan is required to include

- a summary of agency activities that will continue and those that will cease;

- an estimate of the time to complete the shutdown, to the nearest half-day;

- the number of employees expected to be on-board (i.e., filled positions) before implementation of the plan; and

- the total number of employees to be retained (i.e., not furloughed), broken out into five categories of exceptions to the Antideficiency Act, including employees (1) who are paid from a resource other than annual appropriations; (2) who are necessary to perform activities expressly authorized by law; (3) who are necessary to perform activities necessarily implied by law; (4) who are necessary to the discharge of the President's constitutional duties and powers; and (5) who are necessary to protect life and property.[38]

After providing this information for the agency as a whole, an agency's plan is required to further break out some of the information by "component" (e.g., a bureau-size entity within a department). OMB's circular also instructs agencies to take personnel actions to release employees according to applicable law and Office of Personnel Management (OPM) regulations. OPM maintains a website with guidance, historical OMB documents, and frequently asked questions about furloughs.[39]

In general, the OMB circular refers to employees who are to be furloughed as "released," and employees who will not be furloughed as "excepted" or "retained." More broadly, officials and observers may employ a variety of personnel-related terms in the context of a government shutdown, many of which begin with the letter "e." For discussion of the term "excepted" and other terms that may be used in practice, see **Box 3**. Notably, some parts of the federal government may employ a term in a way that is official but different from usage elsewhere. At other times, usage of a term may be colloquial or may suggest meanings that are not intended.

---

[37] OMB, *Circular No. A-11*, July 2014, Section 124.1.

[38] OMB provided guidance to help agencies interpret categories like these in memoranda that were issued during the near-impasses on FY2011 and FY2012 appropriations and the actual impasse on FY2014 appropriations. See, respectively: OMB Memorandum M-11-13, *Planning for Agency Operations During a Lapse in Government Funding*, April 7, 2011, pp. 4-6 (corresponding to FY2011 appropriations); OMB Memorandum M-12-03, *Planning for Agency Operations During a Lapse in Government Funding*, December 15, 2011, Attachment 1 (first three pages of non-paginated attachment) (corresponding to FY2012); and OMB Memorandum M-13-22, *Planning for Agency Operations During a Potential Lapse in Appropriations*, September 17, 2013, pp. 3-5 (corresponding to FY2014).

[39] See U.S. Office of Personnel Management (hereinafter OPM), "Pay & Leave Furlough Guidance," at http://www.opm.gov/policy-data-oversight/pay-leave/furlough-guidance/#url=Shutdown-Furlough.

Box 3. Making Sense of Personnel-Related Terms: Four that Begin with "E"

Excepted. In the executive branch, and in the context of a funding gap, the term "excepted" may refer to (1) the government activities that that must continue during a funding gap and (2) the federal employees who are not furloughed and who must continue to come to work during a funding gap. Consequently, observers and practitioners may refer to both "excepted activities" and "excepted personnel." Intuition for this usage comes from the possibility that some activities and personnel may, by law, be "excepted" from the Antideficiency Act's general prohibitions on continued activity during a funding gap. The legislative and judicial branches are not guided officially by executive branch *documents* regarding the Antideficiency Act's exceptions and related terms. However, they continue to be guided by the Constitution and the act itself, and may look to executive branch guidelines as a point of reference.

Exempt. Some agencies have used the term "exempt" as a synonym for "excepted."[40] Separately, for purposes of general usage across the executive branch, OPM defines "exempt" as referring to employees who are not subject to furlough, because the employees' compensation is not funded by annually appropriated funds.[41]

Emergency. In the executive branch, the term "emergency" generally is not used in the context of shutdowns, in practice.[42] Rather, this term primarily is used in the context of a need for continuity of operations (COOP) in certain situations, such as severe weather conditions, air pollution, power failures, interruption of public transportation, natural disasters, and other situations when significant numbers of employees are prevented from reporting to work or when agencies need to cease all or part of their activities.[43] So-called "emergency employees" are the employees who must report for work notwithstanding these situations.

Essential. News media sometimes use the term "essential" instead of "excepted." In the legislative branch, at least one source has referred to non-furloughed employees as "essential," although this terminology was not used consistently across the branch and may have varied across offices and agencies.[44] In the executive branch, this term was used similarly in the early 1980s.[45] Since then, the term gradually has disappeared from official use in the executive branch in favor of "excepted," in part to prevent a colloquial interpretation of the term "essential" as referring to relative importance or value. In congressional hearings that focused on the first FY1996 shutdown, some witnesses regretted that the terms "nonessential" and "essential" had been used to describe employees subject to furlough, and not subject to furlough, respectively. Use of the term "nonessential" was a misnomer and demeaning, they said.[46]

---

[40] For example, see related discussion in CRS Report R43252, *FY2014 Appropriations Lapse and the Department of Homeland Security: Impact and Legislation*, by William L. Painter.

[41] OPM, *Guidance for Shutdown Furloughs*, October 11, 2013, p. 2, at http://www.opm.gov/policy-data-oversight/pay-leave/furlough-guidance/#url=Shutdown-Furlough.

[42] Nevertheless, the Antideficiency Act itself uses the term "emergencies" in identifying the circumstance when the human life and property exception may be used to allow an agency to except employees from furlough even in the absence of appropriations ("may not... employ personal services exceeding that authorized by law except for *emergencies* involving the safety of human life or the protection of property" (31 U.S.C. §1342; emphasis added)).

[43] OPM, *Guidance for Shutdown Furloughs*, October 11, 2013, p. 2. In a separate guidance document, OPM does not provide standard definitions of "emergency" employees. Due to the diversity of agency missions and workforces, OPM leaves these designations to the discretion of agency heads, based on each agency's mission and circumstances. See OPM, *Washington, DC, Area Dismissal and Closure Procedures*, December 2013, p. 8, at http://www.opm.gov/policy-data-oversight/pay-leave/reference-materials/handbooks/.

[44] For an illustration of use of the term "essential," see U.S. Congress, House Committee on House Administration, *Legislative Operations During a Lapse in Appropriations: Guidance Issued by the Committee on House Administration*, 113th Cong., 1st sess., September 2013, at http://cha.house.gov/lapse-in-appropriations-guidance. In addition, in recent decades, Congress has used the term "essential" when it passed legislation to ratify and approve agencies' past actions to continue performing excepted activities during a funding gap, the performance of which incurred obligations. See the example in the section of this report entitled "General Practices Regarding Furloughs and Pay" (which says "All obligations incurred... for the purposes of maintaining the *essential* level of activity to protect life and property... are hereby ratified and approved" (P.L. 113-46, Section 115(c); emphasis added)).

[45] For example, see OMB Memorandum, *Agency Operations in the Absence of Appropriations*, November 17, 1981.

[46] See U.S. Congress, House Committee on Government Reform and Oversight, Subcommittee on Civil Service, *Government Shutdown I: What's Essential?*, hearings, 104th Cong., 1st sess., December 6 and 14, 1995 (Washington, DC: GPO, 1997), pp. 48, 228-229, at http://www.gpo.gov/fdsys/pkg/CHRG-104hhrg23275/pdf/CHRG-104hhrg23275.pdf.

Aside from *Circular No. A-11*, other OMB documents and guidance from previous funding gaps and shutdowns may provide insights into current and future practices. OPM provides access to previous OMB bulletins and memoranda for reference on its website.[47] Some of these OMB documents also have been reproduced in legislative branch documents.[48]

Detailed Guidance to Agencies and Posting of Shutdown Plans

In addition to OMB's annual instructions in *Circular No. A-11*, OMB may provide more detailed guidance to agencies in specific situations. These formalized communications typically occur through bulletins or memoranda. The documents may be issued to agencies in at least two ways:

- through means that are internal to the executive branch and that generally are not readily visible elsewhere (e.g., posting on an OMB-administered website that cannot be readily accessed outside the executive branch),[49] and

---

[47] See OPM, "Pay & Leave Furlough Guidance," at http://www.opm.gov/policy-data-oversight/pay-leave/furlough-guidance/#url=Shutdown-Furlough. The OMB documents include, in chronological order:

(1) OMB Bulletin No. 80-14, *Shutdown of Agency Operations Upon Failure by the Congress to Enact Appropriations*, August 28, 1980 (citing the 1980 Civiletti opinion and requiring agencies to develop shutdown plans);

(2) OMB Memorandum, *Agency Operations in the Absence of Appropriations*, November 17, 1981 (referencing OMB Bulletin No. 80-14; saying the 1981 Civiletti opinion remains in effect; and providing examples of "excepted activities" that may be continued under a funding gap);

(3) OMB Bulletin No. 80-14, Supplement No. 1, *Agency Operations in the Absence of Appropriations*, August 20, 1982 ("updating" OMB Bulletin No. 80-14 and newly requiring agencies to submit contingency plans for review by OMB);

(4) OMB Memorandum M-91-02, *Agency Operations in the Absence of Appropriations*, October 5, 1990 (referencing OMB Bulletin No. 80-14; stating that OMB Bulletin No. 80-14 was "amended" by the OMB Memorandum of November 17, 1981; saying the 1981 Civiletti opinion remains in effect; and directing agencies on a Friday how to handle a funding gap that begins during the weekend);

(5) OMB Memorandum M-95-18, *Agency Plans for Operations During Funding Hiatus*, August 22, 1995 (referencing OMB Bulletin No. 80-14, as amended; citing the 1981 Civiletti opinion; transmitting to agencies the 1995 OLC opinion as an "update" to the 1981 Civiletti opinion; and directing agencies to send updated contingency plans to OMB);

(6) OMB *Circular No. A-11*, Section 124, July 2014 (providing annually issued guidance to agencies on shutdown-related topics; the Web link currently is mislabeled as corresponding to the August 2011 version of the circular); and

(7) OMB Memorandum M-13-22, *Planning for Agency Operations During a Potential Lapse in Appropriations*, September 17, 2013 (referring to *Circular No. A-11*, OLC legal opinions, and OPM Web guidance; providing detailed directions on what to do during the coming days in the context of FY2014 appropriations negotiations; and providing additional guidance on exceptions to the Antideficiency Act, contracts, grants, information technology, travel, conducting an "orderly shutdown," and payment to excepted employees for time worked).

[48] See U.S. Congress, Senate Committee on the Budget and House Committee on the Budget, *Effects of Potential Government Shutdown*, hearing, 104th Cong., 1st sess., September 19, 1995, S.Hrg. 104-175 (Washington, DC: GPO, 1995), pp. 77-85; GAO, *Funding Gaps Jeopardize Federal Government Operations*, Appendices V, VI, and VII; and U.S. Congress, House Committee on Government Reform and Oversight, Subcommittee on Civil Service, *Government Shutdown I: What's Essential?*, hearings, 104th Cong., 1st sess., December 6 and 14, 1995 (Washington, DC: GPO, 1997), pp. 99-112, 121-131, and 428-430.

[49] See OMB, "MAX.gov Homepage," at https://max.omb.gov/maxportal/. The *MAX.gov* website provides access to several underlying applications on which many categories of documents are now available only to personnel inside the executive branch with a password and permission. Beginning in the 2000s, OMB increasingly used this approach to provide direction to executive branch agencies as well as share information with, and collect information from, agencies. The change in practice became possible after the proliferation of Web-based systems that provide access to a website only to certain organizations or individuals. Previously, OMB sent documents to agencies in hard copy or by email, or placed them on the publicly available World Wide Web. At that earlier time, OMB also operated electronic budget systems that collectively were referred to as the "MAX system," focusing on a narrower purpose of producing (continued...)

- through publicly visible means (e.g., posting a memorandum on OMB's public website).[50]

Documents in the second, publicly visible category may allude to other, non-public guidance. On occasion, Members of Congress have questioned the rationales for how determinations of "excepted" status were made. (See the section of this report that is titled "Quality and Specificity of Agency Planning.") Consequently, it is conceivable that non-public guidance documents might be of interest to Congress in some circumstances.

Both of the aforementioned kinds of communications have been in evidence in the context of shutdown planning. For example, in the days leading up to near-impasses on appropriations for FY2011 and FY2012, OMB supplemented its annual *Circular No. A-11* instructions with more detailed guidance to agencies. Shortly before FY2011 funding was scheduled to expire in April 2011, OMB instructed agencies through a publicly available memorandum to create or revise shutdown plans and post them on the Internet.[51] In these instructions, OMB said it earlier had been "providing guidance and coordinating the efforts of the Executive Branch to facilitate appropriate contingency planning in accordance with the provisions of the Antideficiency Act."[52] OMB apparently provided the earlier guidance and coordination over a period of time through non-public documents and instructions.[53]

For the near-impasses of FY2011 and FY2012, as well as the actual impasse of FY2014, agencies and OMB followed generally the same process of posting shutdown plans on the Internet. In each instance, OMB posted agencies' plans on the same Web page.[54] Many agencies also created their own Web pages, which described shutdown procedures and linked to their plans. These resources covered many topics in addition to the information that OMB *Circular No. A-11* addressed. Additional topics included shutdown precedents, guidelines, furlough policies, and frequently asked questions. Documents also addressed availability of government services, unemployment compensation for federal employees, union concerns, and information about past shutdowns.

(...continued)

the President's annual budget proposal. For discussion of the earlier version, see Shelley Lynne Tomkin, *Inside OMB: Politics and Process in the President's Budget Office* (Armonk, NY: M.E. Sharpe, 1998), p. 17.

[50] To find these documents, see OMB, "Agency Information," at http://www.whitehouse.gov/omb/agency/default.

[51] The issuance occurred a single day before funding from an interim CR was due to expire at the end of the day on April 8, 2011. See OMB, Memorandum M-11-13, *Planning for Agency Operations During a Lapse in Government Funding*, April 7, 2011.

[52] For the quoted text, see ibid., p. 1. The next day, on April 8, 2011, OMB began to post on its website links to the shutdown plans that agencies and the Executive Office of the President had developed under the July 2010 version of *Circular No. A-11*. The potential impasse was avoided before midnight with enactment of another interim CR (P.L. 112-8) and an announcement that the outline of an agreement had been reached on how to provide full-year funding for FY2011.

[53] Several months later, in the context of a near-impasse on FY2012 appropriations, a similar process unfolded. On December 15, 2011, OMB issued a publicly accessible memorandum to agencies related to a potential lapse in FY2012 funding. The memorandum appeared to follow up on prior, non-public instructions. See OMB Memorandum M-12-03, *Planning for Agency Operations During a Lapse in Government Funding*, December 15, 2011, p. 1. OMB also posted revised shutdown plans from many agencies on its website on the same day. The FY2012 funding was scheduled to expire at the end of the day on December 16, 2011. In the context of FY2014 appropriations, OMB issued a similar memorandum two weeks prior to the beginning of FY2014. See OMB Memorandum M-13-22, *Planning for Agency Operations During a Potential Lapse in Appropriations*, September 17, 2013.

[54] OMB, "Agency Contingency Plans," at http://www.whitehouse.gov/omb/contingency-plans.

For FY2014, agencies implemented their plans after OMB instructed them to do so. On September 30, 2013, OMB said in a memorandum that it did not have a clear indication that Congress would act in time for the President to sign a CR before the end of October 1. OMB therefore directed agencies to execute their plans for an "orderly shutdown."[55]

Effects of a Federal Government Shutdown on Government Operations

Effects of a shutdown may occur at various times, including in anticipation of a potential funding gap (e.g., planning), during an actual gap (e.g., furlough and curtailed operations), and afterwards (e.g., addressing backlogs of work). The following sections discuss potential effects of a shutdown from three perspectives:

- effects on federal officials and employees;

- examples of excepted activities and personnel; and

- effects on government operations and services to the public.[56]

Effects on Federal Officials and Employees

General Practices Regarding Furloughs and Pay

An immediate shutdown effect is the "shutdown furlough" of certain federal employees—that is, placement of the employees in a temporary, nonduty, nonpay status.[57] Shutdown furloughs are not considered a break in service and are generally creditable for retaining benefits and seniority. With regard to pay, there appears to be no guarantee that employees placed on shutdown furlough would receive pay for the time they are placed on furlough. This may be the case, because if furloughed employees are prohibited from coming to work during a shutdown, the government arguably would not be incurring a legal obligation to pay them. Several considerations, including personnel costs, future productivity, and employee retention, might be weighed when assessing the issue of retroactive pay for furloughed staff. Nevertheless, in historical practice, federal employees who were furloughed under a shutdown generally have received their salaries

---

[55] OMB Memorandum M-13-24, *Update on Status of Operations*, September 30, 2013.

[56] A government shutdown also may affect the economy. Some of these potential effects are covered in another CRS report, which focused specifically on the FY2014 shutdown. See CRS Report R43292, *The FY2014 Government Shutdown: Economic Effects*, by Marc Labonte.

[57] For more information about shutdown furloughs, see OPM, "Pay & Leave: Furlough Guidance," at http://www.opm.gov/policy-data-oversight/pay-leave/furlough-guidance/#url=Shutdown-Furlough. This OPM website provides detailed questions and answers about shutdown furloughs in a PDF document titled *Guidance for Shutdown Furloughs*. The website also explains the distinction between shutdown furloughs and another type of furlough: "administrative furloughs." In brief, a shutdown furlough occurs when there is a funding gap. An affected agency would need to shut down any activities funded by annual appropriations that are not excepted by law from the Antideficiency Act's prohibitions. An administrative furlough, by contrast, is a planned event by an agency that is designed to absorb reductions necessitated by downsizing, reduced funding, lack of work, or any budget situation other than a funding gap. Furloughs that result from budget sequestration, for example, would be considered administrative furloughs. For more information about sequestration, see CRS Report R42972, *Sequestration as a Budget Enforcement Process: Frequently Asked Questions*, by Megan S. Lynch.

---

retroactively as a result of legislation to that effect.[58] For example, a CR provision required that employees who were furloughed during the FY2014 government shutdown be paid retroactively:

> Employees furloughed as a result of any lapse in appropriations which begins on or about October 1, 2013, shall be compensated at their standard rate of compensation, for the period of such lapse in appropriations, as soon as practicable after such lapse in appropriations ends.[59]

In the case of excepted employees, OMB has stated several times in detailed, shutdown-related guidance to agencies that

> [w]ithout further specific direction or enactment by Congress, all excepted employees are entitled to receive payment for obligations incurred by their agencies for their performance of excepted work during the period of the appropriations lapse. After appropriations are enacted, payroll centers will pay all excepted employees for time worked.[60]

In addition, a 1981 memorandum from OMB to the heads of executive departments and agencies included the following statements:

> It should be made clear that, during a [sic] appropriations hiatus, funds may not be available to permit agency *payment* of obligations. All personnel performing excepted services, including activities incident to the orderly suspension of agency operations, should be assured that the United States will not contest its legal obligation to make payment for such services, even in the absence of appropriations.[61]

Historically, Congress has authorized retroactive pay for excepted employees who work during a government shutdown by ratifying and approving the obligations incurred in anticipation of appropriations. For example, the CR that was enacted following the FY2014 shutdown included the following provision:

---

[58] CRS is not aware of past instances to the contrary.

[59] P.L. 113-46, Section 115(a), 127 Stat. 561, October 17, 2013. A similar provision was enacted after the first FY1996 shutdown. See P.L. 104-56, Section 124, 109 Stat. 553, November 20, 1995. The latter provision was extended by P.L. 104-94, which applied to the second FY1996 shutdown period (110 Stat. 25, January 6, 1996). Separate legislation explicitly said all officers and employees of the federal government and the District of Columbia were deemed to be excepted employees from December 15, 1995, through January 26, 1996, during and beyond the second shutdown period (P.L. 104-92, Section 310). It should be noted that affected employees did not receive compensation until funding for their agencies resumed.

[60] See OMB Memorandum M-11-13, *Planning for Agency Operations During a Lapse in Government Funding*, April 7, 2011, p. 16; OMB Memorandum M-12-03, *Planning for Agency Operations During a Lapse in Government Funding*, December 15, 2011, Attachment 1 (last two pages of non-paginated attachment); and, for the text excerpted above, OMB Memorandum M-13-22, *Planning for Agency Operations During a Potential Lapse in Appropriations*, September 17, 2013, pp. 15-16.

[61] OMB Memorandum, *Agency Operations in the Absence of Appropriations*, Nov. 17, 1981, p. 2-3 (emphasis in original), available at http://www.opm.gov/policy-data-oversight/pay-leave/furlough-guidance/attachment_a-4.pdf. See also American Federation of Government Employees, et al. v. Rivlin, Civil Action No. 95-2115 (EGS), 1995 WL 697236 (D.D.C.), p. *4 (in a lawsuit brought in November 1995 by unions representing groups of federal employees who were compelled by OMB to work without compensation during a government shutdown, the federal district court, in denying a request for a temporary restraining order, observed that "it is purely speculative... whether anyone will ever be denied a paycheck for services rendered during this budgetary impasse. Moreover, in the past, when the government has shut down due to an impasse over the budget, Congress has always appropriated funds to compensate government employees for their services rendered.").

> All obligations incurred in anticipation of the appropriations made and authority granted by this joint resolution for the purposes of maintaining the essential level of activity to protect life and property and bringing about orderly termination of Government functions, and for purposes as otherwise authorized by law, are hereby ratified and approved if otherwise in accord with the provisions of this joint resolution.[62]

Congress and the President have taken this approach before the FY1996 and FY2014 shutdowns, as well. For example, Congress and President Ronald W. Reagan provided retroactive pay to both furloughed and non-furloughed federal employees after a brief funding gap in FY1985.[63]

Extent of Furloughs During the FY1996 and FY2014 Shutdowns

The experiences of FY1996 and FY2014 illustrate what may occur with respect to furloughs during a shutdown of relatively long duration.[64] Among other things, this history shows how the extent of furloughs during a funding gap is driven in large part by the number and composition of regular appropriations bills that remain unenacted during that time period.

Two FY1996 Shutdowns[65]

As noted earlier, two separate funding gaps and corresponding shutdowns occurred in FY1996. A graphical depiction of the FY1996 appropriations process, including the two funding gaps, is available in another CRS report.[66] The first shutdown, which lasted five full days between November 13-19, 1995, resulted in the furlough of approximately 800,000 federal employees in agencies funded by 10 of the then-13 regular appropriations bills.[67] The shutdown was caused by the expiration of a continuing resolution agreed to on September 30, 1995 (P.L. 104-31), and by

---

[62] P.L. 113-46, Section 115(c), 127 Stat. 561, October 17, 2013. A similar provision was enacted after the first FY1996 shutdown. See P.L. 104-56, Section 124, 109 Stat. 553, November 20, 1995. Later, P.L. 104-94 extended this provision to cover the second FY1996 shutdown period (110 Stat. 25, January 6, 1996). Separate legislation explicitly provided FY1996 funding, through January 26, 1996, for salaries of employees who were excepted from furlough and who worked during either of the shutdown periods on projects and activities that were continuing from the previous fiscal year (P.L. 104-92, Section 301, 110 Stat. 19).

[63] P.L. 98-461, 98 Stat. 1814, October 10, 1984.

[64] Between the issuance of the Civiletti opinions in 1980-1981 and 1995, funding gaps were limited to three or fewer full days of duration. Consequently, they were of relatively short duration compared to those of FY1996 and FY2014.

[65] This section was prepared by Jessica Tollestrup, Analyst on Congress and the Legislative Process (jtollestrup@crs.loc.gov, 7-0941) with contributions from Clinton T. Brass, Specialist in Government Organization and Management (cbrass@crs.loc.gov, 7-4536). The section also draws on CRS Report RS20348, *Federal Funding Gaps: A Brief Overview*, by Jessica Tollestrup, and CRS Report 95-906, *Shutdown of the Federal Government: Effects on the Federal Workforce And Other Sectors*, by James P. McGrath (September 25, 1997; out of print, available on request).

[66] CRS Report RS20348, *Federal Funding Gaps: A Brief Overview*, by Jessica Tollestrup.

[67] The figure of 800,000 federal employees was frequently cited at the time. For example, see U.S. Congress, House Committee on Government Reform and Oversight, Subcommittee on Civil Service, *Government Shutdown I: What's Essential?*, hearings, 104th Cong., 1st sess., December 6 and 14, 1995 (Washington, DC: GPO, 1997), pp. 6 and 265; and U.S. President (Clinton), The White House, Office of the Press Secretary, "Statement by the President," November 19, 1995, at http://clinton6.nara.gov/1995/11/1995-11-19-president-statement-on-signing-appropriations-bills.html. As of November 13, three of the 13 regular appropriations acts for FY1996 had been enacted: the Military Construction Appropriations Act (P.L. 104-32), the Agriculture, Rural Development, Food and Drug Administration, and Related Agencies Appropriations Act (P.L. 104-37), and the Energy and Water Development Appropriations Act (P.L. 104-46). Therefore, 10 regular appropriations bills remained unenacted at the start of the first shutdown. The Department of Transportation and Related Agencies Appropriations Act (P.L. 104-50) was enacted after the first full day of the first shutdown, leaving nine regular bills unenacted during the remainder of the first shutdown.

President William J. Clinton's veto of a second continuing resolution.[68] As of December 15, 1995, four additional regular appropriations acts for FY1996 had been enacted.[69] Therefore, six regular appropriations bills remained unenacted at the start of the second shutdown.[70] The second shutdown lasted 21 full days between December 15, 1995, and January 6, 1996.[71] It was triggered by the expiration of a continuing resolution that had been enacted on November 20, 1995 (P.L. 104-56), which funded the government through December 15, 1995. On January 2, 1996, the estimate of furloughed federal employees for the second shutdown was 284,000.[72] Fewer employees and agencies were affected, because some funding bills were enacted during and after the first shutdown, and before the second shutdown. In addition, many employees were recalled back to work even in the absence of funding, due to ongoing redeterminations of employees' status as excepted or non-excepted.[73] There was a total of eight continuing resolutions from January 6, 1996, until April 26, 1996, when the Omnibus Consolidated Rescissions and Appropriations Act of 1996 (P.L. 104-134) was enacted. This consolidated appropriations act provided budget authority for agencies and programs not covered in the FY1996 annual appropriations acts that had become law earlier.

The FY2014 Shutdown

After the second FY1996 shutdown, no shutdowns occurred until over 17 years later, in FY2014.[74] In this case, a funding gap began on October 1, 2013, the first day of FY2014, after funding from the previous fiscal year expired at the end of the day on September 30. At that time, none of the 12 regular appropriations bills for FY2014 had been enacted. On September 30, OMB said in a memorandum that it did not expect a resumption of funding from annual appropriations by the end of the day on October 1.[75] Consequently, OMB instructed the affected agencies to begin the process of ceasing operations and furloughing personnel on October 1.

On September 30, however, an automatic continuing resolution (ACR) was enacted to provide funding for a narrow category of activities at the Departments of Defense (DOD) and Homeland

---

[68] H.J.Res. 115. A measure that would have temporarily increased the debt limit, H.R. 2586, also was vetoed on November 13, 1995.

[69] In addition to the Department of Transportation and Related Agencies Appropriations Act, described in an earlier footnote, these included the Treasury, Postal Service, and General Government Appropriations Act (P.L. 104-52); the Legislative Branch Appropriations Act (P.L. 104-53); and the Department of Defense Appropriations Act (P.L. 104-61).

[70] These included the (1) Department of Interior and Related Agencies Appropriations Act, (2) Department of Veterans Affairs and Housing and Urban Development, and Independent Agencies Appropriations Act, (3) Department of Commerce and Related Agencies Appropriations Act, (4) Foreign Operations, Export Financing, and Related Programs Appropriations Act, (5) Departments of Labor, Health and Human Services, and Education, and Related Agencies Appropriations Act, and (6) District of Columbia Appropriations Act.

[71] For the District of Columbia, full-year funding for certain purposes was provided via a CR during the second shutdown (P.L. 104-69), but final action on annual appropriations superseded that funding (P.L. 104-134).

[72] Another 475,000 excepted federal employees continued to work in nonpay status.

[73] For discussion of the experience of the Social Security Administration, see the relevant discussion in the section of this report titled "Effects on Mandatory Spending Programs."

[74] For more detailed discussion of the appropriations process for FY2014, see CRS Report R43338, *Congressional Action on FY2014 Appropriations Measures*, by Jessica Tollestrup. For an annotated listing of CRS resources related to the FY2014 shutdown, see CRS Report R43250, *CRS Resources on the FY2014 Funding Gap, Shutdown, and Status of Appropriations*, by Justin Murray.

[75] OMB Memorandum M-13-24, *Update on Status of Operations*, September 30, 2013.

Security (DHS).[76] This narrow CR provided funds for FY2014 pay and allowances for certain members of the armed forces and supporting contractors and civilian personnel. Full implementation of the law was delayed several days while agencies determined how to interpret and implement its provisions. The experience may be of interest if similar legislation were considered in anticipation of a potential future shutdown (see **Box 4**).

Box 4. Example of Operating During a Shutdown Under a Narrow CR[77]

The Pay Our Military Act (POMA, P.L. 113-39) was enacted on September 30, 2013, in an effort to mitigate some effects of a shutdown on certain personnel and operations of the "armed forces," which include the Army, Navy, Air Force, and Marine Corps, and, within DHS, the Coast Guard.[78] This legislation was structured as an automatic continuing resolution to provide funding for FY2014 pay and allowances for three categories of personnel: (1) members of the armed forces in "active service"; (2) certain DOD and DHS civilian personnel "providing support" to these armed forces members; and (3) certain DOD and DHS contractors "providing support" to the armed forces members. As such, the act's intended effects apparently were to ensure that (1) covered government personnel who were anticipated to be furloughed during a funding gap would, under POMA, avoid furlough, and (2) all covered individuals would be paid (including government personnel and contractors performing POMA-covered, but non-excepted activities) and, in addition, would be paid on time rather than wait for retroactive pay after enactment of interim or full-year appropriations. Upon POMA's enactment, DOJ worked with DOD and DHS to determine how to interpret and implement the legislation. A DOD official said that DOJ advised that the law did not allow the departments to end furloughs for all civilian employees or pay all contractors.[79] Rather, specific determinations would be necessary. Consequently, DOD and DHS did not initially avoid furloughs for the first few days of the shutdown for any of their POMA-covered, non-excepted employees, because the determinations reportedly took time to make.[80]

On October 5, 2013, DHS and DOD announced the general parameters under which they would bring employees back to work and pay contractors during the week of Monday, October 7. For example, DOD Comptroller Robert F. Hale said the department had "roughly" 350,000 employees on furlough, and that under POMA, "my guess is that we'll bring most of them back but no more than a few tens of thousands will remain on furlough, and it may be substantially less than that." Mr. Hale also "offer[ed] one final note of caution about this recall," saying "we have authority to recall most of our civilians and provide them pay and allowances. We don't have authority to enter into obligations for supplies, parts, fuel, et cetera unless it is for an excepted activity, again, one tied to a military operation or safety of life and property. So as our people come back to work, they'll need to be careful that they do not order supplies and material for non-excepted activities."

Ultimately, the FY2014 shutdown lasted 16 full days, through the end of October 16. The funding gap terminated when the President signed an interim CR in the early morning of Thursday, October 17, 2013 (P.L. 113-46).

During the first week of October, information about furloughs occasionally was reported by the news media. Initial reports suggested that 800,000 or more executive branch employees had been

---

[76] P.L. 113-39, 127 Stat. 532, September 30, 2013. Typically, an ACR is intended to ensure that a source of funding is available at a specified level, without further need for legislation, for one or more discretionary spending activities in the event that the timely enactment of appropriations is disrupted. The concept of an ACR has been both applauded and criticized. For further information about P.L. 113-39 and the general topic of ACRs, see CRS Report R41948, *Automatic Continuing Resolutions: Background and Overview of Recent Proposals*, by Jessica Tollestrup.

[77] For more detailed discussion, see CRS Report R41948, *Automatic Continuing Resolutions: Background and Overview of Recent Proposals*, by Jessica Tollestrup; CRS Report R43252, *FY2014 Appropriations Lapse and the Department of Homeland Security: Impact and Legislation*, by William L. Painter; and CRS Report R41745, *Government Shutdown: Operations of the Department of Defense During a Lapse in Appropriations*, by Amy Belasco and Pat Towell.

[78] P.L. 113-39, Section 2(a)(1), which explicitly referred to the definition of "armed forces" at 10 U.S.C. §101(a)(4).

[79] U.S. Department of Defense, "Press Briefing on the Secretary of Defense's Interpretation of the Pay Our Military Act," news transcript, October 5, 2013, at http://www.defense.gov/Transcripts/Transcript.aspx?TranscriptID=5320.

[80] This information and the subsequent quotes in **Box 4** come from ibid.

furloughed, based on the contents of agency shutdown plans.[81] Three weeks after the shutdown terminated, OMB released a retrospective report.[82] According to OMB, the shutdown resulted in the furlough "roughly 850,000 employees per day" at its peak in the first few days of October, or approximately 40% of the federal civilian workforce.[83] The number decreased during the course of the shutdown due to the implementation of P.L. 113-39 (see **Box 4**). In addition, the total number of furloughs varied over time, due to the net effect of ongoing redeterminations regarding whether an employee's status as excepted or non-excepted should change in response to a change in an agency's circumstances.[84]

For the shutdowns of FY1996 and FY2014, OMB did not issue an overall estimate of the number of furloughs across all three branches of the federal government. A look at furlough and pay practices across the three branches, however, may provide further insights into the potential effects of a shutdown on federal officials and employees.

Selected Furlough and Pay Practices, by Branch of Government

Executive Branch[85]

Among the three branches of the federal government, the executive branch is the largest in number of personnel and size of budgets. Several types of executive branch officials and employees are not subject to furlough. These include the President, certain presidential appointees, and federal employees deemed "excepted."[86] OPM has described "excepted"

---

[81] For example, see ABC News, "Government Shutdown: By the Numbers," *ABCnews.com*, September 30, 2013, at http://abcnews.go.com/Politics/government-shutdown-numbers/story?id=20424204.

[82] The report was posted on OMB's blog. See OMB, "Impacts and Costs of the October 2013 Federal Government Shutdown," November 7, 2013, at http://www.whitehouse.gov/blog/2013/11/07/impacts-and-costs-government-shutdown; and, for the report itself, OMB, *Impacts and Costs of the October 2013 Federal Government Shutdown*, November 2013, at http://www.whitehouse.gov/sites/default/files/omb/reports/impacts-and-costs-of-october-2013-federal-government-shutdown-report.pdf.

[83] Ibid., p. 13. This tally included only the executive branch. Conversation with OMB official, January 3, 2014.

[84] OMB, *Impacts and Costs of the October 2013 Federal Government Shutdown*, November 2013, pp. 13-14, and Josh Hicks, "Agencies Increasingly Calling Back Furloughed Workers," October 11, 2013, *Washington Post*, p. A18.

[85] This section was prepared by Clinton T. Brass, Specialist in Government Organization and Management (cbrass@crs.loc.gov, 7-4536), and Brian T. Yeh, Legislative Attorney (byeh@crs.loc.gov, 7-5182).

[86] For discussion, see GAO, *Principles of Federal Appropriations Law*, 3rd ed., vol. II, pp. 6-149 - 6-150. According to OPM, individuals appointed by the President—including both Senate-confirmed and non-Senate-confirmed—who are not subject to Chapter 63 of Title 5, *U.S. Code* (5 U.S.C. §6301 et seq.), relating to annual and sick leave or to an equivalent formal leave system, are not subject to furlough. OPM has explained that

> [t]hese leave-exempt Presidential appointees are not subject to furloughs because they are considered to be entitled to the pay of their offices solely by virtue of their status as an officer, rather than by virtue of the hours they work. In other words, their compensation is attached to their office, and, by necessary implication of the President's authority to appoint such employees, their service under such an appointment creates budgetary obligations without the need for additional statutory authorization. Based on opinions of the Office of Legal Counsel, Department of Justice, the Antideficiency Act prohibition on creating a budgetary obligation before an appropriation is made is not applicable if the obligation is otherwise "authorized by law."

OPM added that "[a] leave-exempt Presidential appointee cannot be placed on nonduty status. Thus, the appointee's pay cannot be reduced based on placement in nonduty status, including via the mechanism of a furlough." However, a presidential appointee who is a member of the Senior Executive Service (SES) or who serves in a "senior level" position for purposes of 5 U.S.C. § 5376 is covered by the Chapter 63 leave system and is subject to furlough in the same manner as other federal employees. See OPM, *Guidance for Shutdown Furloughs*, October 11, 2013, pp. 1 and 2- (continued...)

---

employees, who are required to work during a shutdown, as "employees who are funded through annual appropriations who are nonetheless excepted from the furlough because they are performing work that, by law, may continue to be performed during a lapse in appropriations."[87] Nevertheless, excepted employees who are normally paid from annual appropriations would not receive pay for time worked during the shutdown period until funding resumes.

With regard to the President's pay, Article II, Section 1 of the Constitution forbids the salary of the President to be reduced while he or she is in office, thus effectively guaranteeing the President of compensation regardless of any shutdown action.[88]

Judicial Branch[89]

During a funding gap, the judiciary would likely be able to continue to operate for a limited time using funds derived from court filings and other fees and from no-year appropriations.[90] For example, in preparation for the FY2014 shutdown, the judiciary estimated that these funds, if used cautiously, could have sustained judiciary activities for approximately 10 working days after an appropriations lapse.[91]

If a lapse in appropriations were to exist after various fee balances like these were exhausted, the judiciary would continue to operate under the terms of the Antideficiency Act, which the judiciary said allows "essential work" to continue during a lapse in appropriations.[92] Such "essential work" includes powers exercised by the judiciary under the Constitution, including activities that support the exercise of Article III judicial powers (i.e., the resolution of cases).[93] Consequently, in the judicial branch, judges would not be subject to furlough, nor would core court staff and probation and pretrial services officers whose service is considered essential to the continued resolution of cases. Each court would be responsible for determining the number of court staff

---

(...continued)

3, at http://www.opm.gov/policy-data-oversight/pay-leave/furlough-guidance/#url=Shutdown-Furlough. In providing this guidance, OPM cited 31 U.S.C. §1341 and an OLC opinion from 2011. See U.S. Department of Justice, Office of Legal Counsel, *Authority to Employ White House Office Personnel Exempt from the Annual and Sick Leave Act Under 5 U.S.C. § 6301(2)(x) and (xi) During an Appropriations Lapse*, memorandum from Karl R. Thompson, Deputy Assistant Attorney General, for the Counsel to the President, April 8, 2011, at http://www.justice.gov/sites/default/files/olc/opinions/2011/04/31/wh-offrs-exempt-from-leave_0.pdf.

[87] See OPM, *Guidance for Shutdown Furloughs*, October 11, 2013, p. 1. OPM refers agencies to DOJ opinions regarding how to determine which employees are designated to be performing excepted or non-excepted functions. OPM added that agency legal counsels and senior agency managers make these determinations.

[88] U.S. Constitution, Article II, §1, cl. 7 ("The President shall, at stated Times, receive for his Services, a Compensation, which shall neither be increased nor diminished during the Period for which he shall have been elected ... ").

[89] This section was prepared by Barry J. McMillion, Analyst on the Federal Judiciary (bmcmillion@crs.loc.gov, 7-6025); Matthew E. Glassman, Analyst on the Congress (mglassman@crs.loc.gov, 7-3467); and Brian T. Yeh, Legislative Attorney (byeh@crs.loc.gov, 7-5182). Denis Steven Rutkus, formerly a Specialist on the Federal Judiciary at CRS, and Lorraine H. Tong, formerly an Analyst in American National Government at CRS, contributed as well.

[90] Administrative Office of the U.S. Courts, Memorandum, *Status of Judiciary Funding and Guidance for Judiciary Operations During a Lapse in Appropriations*, September 24, 2013, p. 3, at http://legaltimes.typepad.com/files/shutdown.pdf.

[91] Ibid.

[92] Ibid.

[93] Ibid.

---

and officers needed to support the exercise of its Article III judicial powers.[94] Such staff performing "essential work" functions would report to work in a non-pay status, while other staff would be furloughed.[95]

Protected by a constitutional prohibition against a diminution in their pay, Supreme Court Justices and other Article III judges would continue to be paid during a lapse in appropriations.[96] Also, in the judiciary's view, other judicial officers, such as U.S. magistrate judges and U.S. bankruptcy judges, may continue to be paid as well.[97] According to the Administrative Office of the U.S. Courts, staff performing "essential functions and working in non-pay status should expect to be paid once" Congress enacts an appropriation, while furloughed judicial staff would not receive compensation unless and until Congress expressly authorized it.[98]

Legislative Branch[99]

During the first FY1996 shutdown and the FY2014 shutdown,[100] the House and Senate continued to engage in many aspects of the legislative process. For example, new legislation was introduced, committees held hearings and markups, reports were filed, legislative business on a variety of policy topics was conducted, and nominations were considered in the Senate. The House and Senate Rules, which govern procedure in each chamber, did not formally address a lapse in appropriations or provide alternative procedures that would be specifically applicable during such periods.

Due to their constitutional responsibilities and a permanent appropriation for congressional pay,[101] Members of Congress are not subject to furlough. Additionally, Article I, Section 6, of the

---

[94] Ibid.

[95] Ibid.

[96] Article III, Section 1 of the Constitution provides that the Supreme Court's Justices and the judges "in such inferior Courts as the Congress may... establish," shall "receive for their Services, a Compensation, which shall not be diminished during the Continuance in office." In addition to Supreme Court Justices, this constitutional provision applies to judges receiving appointment to the U.S. District Courts, U.S. Circuit Courts of Appeals, and U.S. Court of International Trade. See Administrative Office of the U.S. Courts, Memorandum, *Status of Judiciary Funding and Guidance for Judiciary Operations During a Lapse in Appropriations,* September 24, 2013, Attachment 1, p. 3 ("Under the Constitution, Article III judges are entitled to their salary and will continue to work regardless of any lapse in appropriations. The judiciary must seek authorization from the Secretary of the Treasury to issue salary payments to Article III judges during a government shutdown.").

[97] Ibid. ("Bankruptcy judges' salaries are fixed by statute (28 U.S.C. § 153); hence, they may not be furloughed without pay and should continue to work during an appropriations lapse. The judiciary must request the Secretary of the Treasury to authorize bankruptcy judges' salaries during a government shutdown. If not authorized, bankruptcy judges' salaries would be paid retroactively upon the enactment of the judiciary's appropriations act.").

[98] Ibid. ("Staff performing essential functions and working in a non-pay status should expect to be paid once appropriations are enacted; Congress will have to take affirmative action to authorize pay for staff who are furloughed.").

[99] This section was prepared by Ida A. Brudnick, Specialist on the Congress (ibrudnick@crs.loc.gov, 7-6460), and Brian T. Yeh, Legislative Attorney (byeh@crs.loc.gov, 7-5182).

[100] The FY1996 legislative branch appropriations act (P.L. 104-53) was enacted prior to the second, 21-full-day, 1995-1996 government shutdown.

[101] A permanent, mandatory appropriation for salaries for Members of the Senate and House of Representatives, the Resident Commissioner from Puerto Rico, the Delegates, and the Vice President, was included in P.L. 97-51; 95 Stat. 966; September 11, 1981 (2 U.S.C. §31 note). See also, for example: "Table 32-1. Federal Programs By Agency and Account" in *Analytical Perspectives, Budget of the United States Government, Fiscal Year 2014* (Washington, GPO: 2013), pp. 2, 3. Additional information regarding compensation for Members of Congress, including votes in the 112th (continued...)

Constitution states that Members of Congress "shall receive a Compensation for their Services, to be ascertained by Law, and paid out of the Treasury of the United States,"[102] and the 27th Amendment states, "No law, varying the compensation for the services of the Senators and Representatives, shall take effect, until an election of Representatives shall have intervened."[103]

During a funding gap, pay for congressional employees would not be disbursed if there is no appropriation to fund legislative branch activities. Any decision regarding requirements that a congressional employee continue to work during a government shutdown would appear to fall to his or her employing authority.[104] Activities of legislative branch agencies would likely also be restricted, in consultation with Congress, to activities required to support Congress with its constitutional responsibilities or those necessary to protect life and property.[105]

Timing of Furloughed Employees' Return to Work After Funding Resumes

When a funding gap concludes due to the resumption of interim or full-year funding, agencies and employees undertake efforts to resume their normal activities consistent with the funding that the legislation provides.[106] The timing of when funding resumes can have implications for how

---

(...continued)

Congress, is available in CRS Report 97-615, *Salaries of Members of Congress: Congressional Votes, 1990-2014*, by Ida A. Brudnick. On this subject, GAO's *Principles of Federal Appropriations Law* states:

> The salary of a Member of Congress is fixed by statute and therefore cannot be waived without specific statutory authority. B-159835, April 22, 1975; B-123424, Mar. 7, 1975; B-123424, Apr. 15, 1955; A-8427, March 19, 1925; B-206396.2, Nov. 15, 1988 (nondecision letter). However, as each of these cases points out, nothing prevents a Senator or Representative from accepting the salary and then, as several have done, donate part or all of it back to the United States Treasury.

See GAO, *Principles of Federal Appropriations Law*, 3rd ed., vol. II, p. 6-105. For example, see the "Summary of General Fund Receipts and Gifts to the United States for Reduction of the Public Debt" section of the quarterly *Statement of Disbursements of the House, as Compiled by the Chief Administrative Officer*, available at http://disbursements house.gov/.

[102] U.S. Constitution, Article I, §6, cl. 1 ("The Senators and Representatives shall receive a Compensation for their Services, to be ascertained by Law, and paid out of the Treasury of the United States.").

[103] The 27th Amendment to the Constitution was proposed on September 25, 1789, and ratified May 7, 1992.

[104] Congressional employing authorities include the following: individual Members of Congress for staff working in personal offices; chairs of individual House, Senate, and joint committees for committee staff; Members who hold leadership positions for staff in their respective leadership offices; and House or Senate officers or officials for staff working in those offices. In April 2011, in the context of deliberations over FY2011 appropriations, the House Committee on House Administration posted related guidance and issued "Dear Colleague" letters. Planning for operations under a lapse of appropriations was also discussed in U.S. Congress, House, *First Semiannual Report on the Activities of the Committee on House Administration*, 112th Cong., 1st sess., H.Rept. 112-137 (Washington, DC: GPO, 2011), pp. 19-20. See also: U.S. Congress, House, *First Annual Report on the Activities of the Committee on House Administration During the One Hundred Thirteenth Congress Together with Minority Views*, 113th Cong., 1st sess., H.Rept. 113-312 (Washington, DC: GPO, 2014), p. 13. The Committee on House Administration posted "Guidance on Legislative Operations During a Lapse in Appropriations" regarding the FY2014 shutdown on October 1, 2013, at http://cha house.gov/lapse-in-appropriations-guidance. The guidance addressed, for example, decisions regarding the retention of employees consistent with the Constitution and the Antideficiency Act. For questions regarding congressional and legislative branch operations, see the "Key Policy Staff" table at the end of this report.

[105] For additional discussion, including the status of legislative branch agencies and personnel, see GAO, *Principles of Federal Appropriations Law*, 3rd ed., vol. II, pp. 6-149 - 6-150; and GAO, Letter from James F. Hinchman, GAO General Counsel, to John J. Kominski, Library of Congress General Counsel, B-241911, October 23, 1990, at http://archive.gao.gov/lglp2pdf23/087761.pdf.

[106] Full-year funding provides an overall level for a budget account within which agencies must constrain their obligations over the duration of the fiscal year. Interim funding through a CR, by contrast, does not provide a level. (continued...)

---

soon agencies and employees are able to resume full operations, however. The shutdowns of FY2014 and FY1996 provide illustrations of this process.

In FY2014, for example, President Barack Obama signed an interim CR to bring the FY2014 shutdown to an end,[107] reportedly shortly after midnight in the morning of Thursday, October 17, 2013.[108] The Administration judged that this timing was early enough to enable a re-opening of the federal government on October 17. Along these lines, OMB issued a memorandum to agencies and reportedly released it to the news media just before 1 a.m. eastern standard time on October 17.[109] In the memorandum, OMB indicated that "[a]ll employees who were on furlough due to the absence of appropriations may now return to work."[110] Separately, OPM posted guidance for executive branch employees on its website at 12:30 a.m. The guidance said employees were "expected to return to work on their next regularly scheduled work day (Thursday, October 17th for most employees), absent other instructions from their employing agencies."[111]

The experience of FY1996 was different. If funding resumes later during a calendar day, there may not be adequate time for an agency or its personnel to resume their activities during the same day. At the conclusion of the first FY1996 shutdown, for example, interim funding was enacted late in the evening on Sunday, November 19, 1995.[112] As a consequence, funding technically was available for operations earlier on that day. In many if not most instances, however, affected agency operations did not restart until the following day, November 20, 1995.[113] In this situation, a five-full-day funding gap may have resulted in a six-day shutdown for affected agencies.

(...continued)

Instead, an interim CR provides authority to obligate and spend funds for an appropriations account at a statutorily prescribed pace, or "rate," over time. An agency may continue to obligate and spend funds at this rate for the duration of the interim CR—that is, until the CR expires or is superseded. For more information, see CRS Report RL34700, *Interim Continuing Resolutions (CRs): Potential Impacts on Agency Operations*, by Clinton T. Brass.

[107] P.L. 113-46.

[108] Jennifer Epstein, "Obama Signs Bill Ending Shutdown, Raising Debt Ceiling," *Politico.com*, October 17, 2013, at http://www.politico.com/politico44/2013/10/obama-signs-bill-ending-shutdown-raising-debt-ceiling-175280 html.

[109] Josh Gerstein, "OMB Issues Back-to-work Order," *Politico.com*, October 17, 2013, at http://www.politico.com/politico44/2013/10/omb-issues-backtowork-memo-175281 html.

[110] OMB also instructed the heads of agencies to "reopen offices in a prompt and orderly manner." OMB Memorandum M-14-01, *Reopening Departments and Agencies*, October 17, 2013.

[111] In this posting, OPM added guidance for agencies as well, saying that "[a]gencies are strongly encouraged to use all available workplace flexibilities to ensure a smooth transition back to work for employees (e.g. telework, work schedule flexibilities, and excused absence for hardship situations)." The guidance was temporarily posted at OPM, "Snow & Dismissal Procedures Current Status," October 17, 2013, https://www.opm.gov/policy-data-oversight/snow-dismissal-procedures/current-status/. The guidance currently is archived at https://www.opm.gov/policy-data-oversight/snow-dismissal-procedures/status-archives/.

[112] According to the Legislative Information System (http://lis.gov/), Congress passed a resumption of funding shortly before 9 p m. on Sunday, November 19, 1995 (P.L. 104-54). The President signed the legislation later that evening.

[113] For example, agency activities that would have operated during daylight hours on November 19 in the absence of a funding gap (e.g., certain National Park Service facilities) presumably continued to be shut down most of the day, even though enactment of the legislation effectively made funding available for operations to resume earlier that day. OMB has not posted most of its memoranda from 1995 on its website, making OMB's guidance regarding the conclusion of the first FY1996 shutdown more difficult to document. Nevertheless, President Clinton indicated at a news conference during the evening of November 19, 1995, that "tomorrow the Government will go back to work." See U.S. National Archives and Records Administration, Office of the Federal Register, *Public Papers of the Presidents of the United States: William J. Clinton*, 1995, vol. 2 (Washington, DC: GPO, 1996), p. 1774.

Apart from the specific events of FY1996 and FY2014, OPM has addressed this matter generally in prospective guidance to agencies, relating to when furloughed employees may be expected to return to work.

> If a shutdown were to occur, guidance concerning when furloughed employees should come back to work at the conclusion of the shutdown would have to be tailored to the specific situation. In the absence of such guidance, agencies should apply a rule of reason in requiring employees to return to work as soon as possible, taking into account the disruption in the lives and routines of furloughed employees that a shutdown causes.[114]

Examples of Excepted Activities and Personnel

Previous determinations of excepted activities and personnel would not necessarily hold for any future shutdown. However, past experience may inform future agency and OMB decisions. Perspectives on this topic might be gleaned from documents associated with shutdowns and near-shutdowns from the past.

Agency Shutdown Plans

Compared to more recent events, the experience of the FY1996 shutdowns is more difficult to document, because the FY1996 events did not result in wide publication on the Internet of agency shutdown plans.[115] The near-impasses in April and December 2011, by contrast, regarding enactment of FY2011 and FY2012 annual appropriations, resulted in executive branch agencies posting a substantial amount of information on the Internet about their plans for a potential shutdown, including information about excepted and non-excepted personnel and activities.[116] In September 2013, in the context of FY2014 annual appropriations, OMB directed agencies to update these plans and prepare for their potential release.[117] These mostly-updated plans ultimately were posted on websites of agencies and OMB.[118] Looking ahead, any of these plans might provide insight into questions of whether government activities at a specific agency or program, and in a specific situation, would continue or cease, at least according to interpretations of law at the time.

---

[114] OPM, *Guidance for Shutdown Furloughs*, October 11, 2013, question P.13., pp. 27-28.

[115] In 1995 and 1996, federal agencies could be characterized as newly using the World Wide Web at the dawn of the Internet, apparently resulting in less information being posted compared to more recent years. In addition, the FY1996 shutdowns were the first relatively lengthy shutdowns to occur after the Civiletti opinions were issued in 1980-1981. Consequently, the sophistication of agencies in planning for shutdowns and documenting those plans probably was not as developed at that time, compared to the sophistication of agencies during the experiences of 2011 and 2014.

[116] These plans were posted on agency websites and also the OMB website. Most of these plans were revised in anticipation of a potential FY2014 shutdown. The FY2011 and FY2012 plans may be available from agencies, if a congressional office were to inquire directly with specific agencies. CRS also has undertaken some effort to capture PDFs of many agency shutdown plans from that time, if related questions were of interest.

[117] OMB Memorandum M-13-22, *Planning for Agency Operations During a Potential Lapse in Appropriations*, September 17, 2013, p. 2.

[118] Plans that were updated for the near-impasses of calendar year 2011 and the actual shutdown of October 2013 were posted at OMB, "Agency Contingency Plans," at http://www.whitehouse.gov/omb/contingency-plans.

OMB Guidance

More generally, OMB memoranda may provide insights into which activities and personnel might be considered to be excepted. In April and December 2011, then-OMB Director Jacob J. Lew outlined several categories of exceptions to the Antideficiency Act and provided further explanation on how agencies should interpret the categories.[119] OMB Director Sylvia M. Burwell provided similar guidance in September 2013.[120] These documents were primarily conceptual in nature and focused on explaining key principles that apply during a funding gap.

Three decades earlier, however, an OMB memorandum of November 17, 1981, from Director David A. Stockman to the heads of executive agencies, identified concrete "examples of excepted activities."[121] The memorandum, which still was in effect for the FY1996 shutdowns and posted online by OPM as a reference for agencies for the FY2014 shutdown, explained:

> Beginning [on the first day of the appropriations hiatus], agencies may continue activities otherwise authorized by law, those that protect life and property and those necessary to begin phasedown of other activities. Primary examples of activities agencies may continue are those which may be found under applicable statutes to:
>
> 1. Provide for the national security, including the conduct of foreign relations essential to the national security or the safety of life and property.
>
> 2. Provide for benefit payments and the performance of contract obligations under no-year or multi-year or other funds remaining available for those purposes.
>
> 3. Conduct essential activities to the extent that they protect life and property, including:
>
>> a. Medical care of inpatients and emergency outpatient care;
>>
>> b. Activities essential to ensure continued public health and safety, including safe use of food and drugs and safe use of hazardous materials;
>>
>> c. The continuance of air traffic control and other transportation safety functions and the protection of transport property;
>>
>> d. Border and coastal protection and surveillance;
>>
>> e. Protection of Federal lands, buildings, waterways, equipment and other property owned by the United States;
>>
>> f. Care of prisoners and other persons in the custody of the United States;

---

[119] OMB Memorandum M-11-13, *Planning for Agency Operations During a Lapse in Government Funding*, April 7, 2011, pp. 4-6; and OMB Memorandum M-12-03, *Planning for Agency Operations During a Lapse in Government Funding*, December 15, 2011, Attachment 1.

[120] OMB Memorandum M-13-22, *Planning for Agency Operations During a Potential Lapse in Appropriations*, September 17, 2013, Attachment 1.

[121] OMB Memorandum, *Agency Operations in the Absence of Appropriations*, November 17, 1981. OPM continues to post this memorandum on the Web page that provides guidance to agencies on shutdown furloughs. See OPM, "Pay & Leave Furlough Guidance," at http://www.opm.gov/policy-data-oversight/pay-leave/furlough-guidance/#url= Shutdown-Furlough.

g. Law enforcement and criminal investigations;

h. Emergency and disaster assistance;

i. Activities essential to the preservation of the essential elements of the money and banking system of the United States, including borrowing and tax collection activities of the Treasury;

j. Activities that ensure production of power and maintenance of the power distribution system; and

k. Activities necessary to maintain protection of research property.

You should maintain the staff and support services necessary to continue these essential functions.

Effects on Government Operations and Services to the Public

The effects of a shutdown on government operations may be examined through multiple and sometimes overlapping perspectives. In the sections below, this report highlights three:

- illustrations of program- or policy-related effects from past shutdowns;

- potential costs associated with a shutdown; and

- general effects of a shutdown on mandatory spending programs.

More detailed discussion of some topics may be found in other CRS products. They discuss the potential effects of a shutdown on government procurement,[122] selected agencies,[123] recipients of federal grants,[124] the economy,[125] and other subjects of potential interest to Congress.[126]

Illustrations of Program- or Policy-Related Effects from Past Shutdowns

Although the effects on the public of any future shutdown would not necessarily reflect past experience, past events may be illustrative of effects that are possible.[127] Several examples follow,

---

[122] CRS Report R42469, *Government Procurement in Times of Fiscal Uncertainty*, by Kate M. Manuel and Erika K. Lunder. This report provides an overview of the various options that the government has, pursuant to the terms of its contracts or otherwise, when confronted with actual or potential funding gaps, funding shortfalls, or budget cuts.

[123] For example, see CRS Report R41745, *Government Shutdown: Operations of the Department of Defense During a Lapse in Appropriations*, by Amy Belasco and Pat Towell; and CRS Report R43252, *FY2014 Appropriations Lapse and the Department of Homeland Security: Impact and Legislation*, by William L. Painter.

[124] CRS Report R43467, *Federal Aid to State and Local Governments: Select Issues Raised by a Federal Government Shutdown*, by Natalie Keegan.

[125] CRS Report R43292, *The FY2014 Government Shutdown: Economic Effects*, by Marc Labonte.

[126] For an annotated list of CRS products that relate to the FY2014 shutdown, see CRS Report R43250, *CRS Resources on the FY2014 Funding Gap, Shutdown, and Status of Appropriations*, by Justin Murray.

[127] In 1981, GAO developed a "hypothetical case" of the possible effects of a 30-day government-wide funding gap and shutdown, which GAO characterized as "unthinkable." After the release of the first Civiletti opinion concerning compliance with the Antideficiency Act, GAO characterized the legal opinion as "fundamentally alter[ing] the environment in which Federal agencies must prepare for a period of expired appropriations." Previously, interpretation of the Antideficiency Act had been much less strict, as noted earlier in this CRS report. The results of GAO's (continued...)

---

below, that were reported by the news media, OMB, and agencies, and in congressional hearings, about the operations and services of federal programs and agencies. The examples focus on the FY1996 and FY2014 shutdowns, in particular.[128]

The Two FY1996 Shutdowns

The effects of the two FY1996 funding gaps and shutdowns received extensive attention. Nevertheless, funding gaps occurred for only some of the then-13 regular appropriations bills. Consequently, the shutdowns' effects were limited primarily to agencies and programs that were included in these bills.[129] Several illustrations of the shutdowns' effects on executive branch agencies and programs are highlighted in the bullets below.[130]

- **Health.** New patients were not accepted into clinical research at the National Institutes of Health (NIH) clinical center; the Centers for Disease Control and Prevention ceased disease surveillance; and hotline calls to NIH concerning diseases were not answered.[131]

- **Law Enforcement and Public Safety.** Delays occurred in the processing of alcohol, tobacco, firearms, and explosives applications by the Bureau of Alcohol, Tobacco, and Firearms; work on more than 3,500 bankruptcy cases reportedly was suspended; cancellation of the recruitment and testing of federal law-enforcement officials reportedly occurred, including the hiring of 400 border patrol agents; and delinquent child-support cases were delayed.[132]

- **Parks, Museums, and Monuments.** Closure of 368 National Park Service sites (loss of 7 million visitors) reportedly occurred, with loss of tourism revenues to local communities; and closure of national museums and monuments (reportedly with an estimated loss of 2 million visitors) occurred.[133]

(...continued)

illustrative survey are available in GAO, *Funding Gaps Jeopardize Federal Government Operations*, pp. 48-56.

[128] For an annotated list of federal government resources that relate to past shutdowns, see CRS Report R41759, *Past Government Shutdowns: Key Resources*, by Jared C. Nagel and Justin Murray.

[129] For a detailed chronology and graphical depiction of which regular appropriations bills were affected by the two funding gaps, see CRS Report RS20348, *Federal Funding Gaps: A Brief Overview*, by Jessica Tollestrup.

[130] The examples are drawn from more extensive discussion in CRS Report 95-906, *Shutdown of the Federal Government: Effects on the Federal Workforce And Other Sectors*, by James P. McGrath (out of print; available upon request). Many of the examples come from media accounts during and after the second shutdown and agency accounts in congressional hearings after the first FY1996 shutdown. For more information, see U.S. Congress, House Committee on Government Reform and Oversight, Subcommittee on Civil Service, *Government Shutdown I: What's Essential?*, hearings, 104th Cong., 1st sess., December 6 and 14, 1995 (Washington, DC: GPO, 1997), at http://www.gpo.gov/fdsys/pkg/CHRG-104hhrg23275/pdf/CHRG-104hhrg23275.pdf.

[131] U.S. Congress, House Committee on Government Reform and Oversight, Subcommittee on Civil Service, *Government Shutdown I: What's Essential?*, hearings, 104th Cong., 1st sess., December 6 and 14, 1995 (Washington, DC: GPO, 1997), p. 23; and Stephen Barr and Frank Swoboda, "Jobless Aid, Toxic Waste Cleanup Halt," *Washington Post*, January 3, 1996, p. A1.

[132] U.S. Congress, House Committee on Government Reform and Oversight, Subcommittee on Civil Service, *Government Shutdown I: What's Essential?*, hearings, 104th Cong., 1st sess., December 6 and 14, 1995 (Washington, DC: GPO, 1997), pp. 62 and 228, at http://www.gpo.gov/fdsys/pkg/CHRG-104hhrg23275/pdf/CHRG-104hhrg23275.pdf; and Stephen Barr and David Montgomery, "At Uncle Sam's No One Answers," *Washington Post*, November 16, 1995, p. A1.

[133] Dan Morgan and Stephen Barr, "When Shutdown Hits Home Ports," *Washington Post*, January 8, 1996, p. A1.

- **Visas and Passports.** Approximately 20,000-30,000 applications by foreigners for visas reportedly went unprocessed each day; 200,000 U.S. applications for passports reportedly went unprocessed; and U.S. tourist industries and airlines reportedly sustained millions of dollars in losses.[134]

- **American Veterans.** Multiple services were curtailed, ranging from health and welfare to finance and travel.[135]

- **Federal Contractors.** Of $18 billion in Washington, DC, area contracts, $3.7 billion (over 20%) reportedly were affected adversely by the funding lapse; the National Institute of Standards and Technology (NIST) was unable to issue a new standard for lights and lamps that was scheduled to be effective January 1, 1996, possibly resulting in delayed product delivery and lost sales; and employees of federal contractors reportedly were furloughed without pay.[136]

OMB briefly summarized the effects of the two FY1996 shutdowns in a two-page February 1996 letter and two short attachments. These documents later were included in a congressional hearing print.[137] OMB identified in one three-page attachment what OMB said were "illustrations" of the effects of the shutdowns. The documents also listed agencies and corresponding numbers of employees who were said to be excepted or not excepted from furlough, and provided an overall cost estimate. The FY1996 cost estimate is discussed in the section of this CRS report titled "Potential Costs Associated with a Shutdown."

During the FY1996 government shutdowns,[138] the federal courts generally operated with limited disruption to their personnel.[139] In the absence of appropriated funds, the judiciary used fee revenues and "carryover" funds from prior years to support what it considered its essential

---

[134] Thomas W. Lippman, "Inconvenience Edges Toward Emergency," *Washington Post*, January 3, 1996, p. A11.

[135] U.S. Congress, House Committee on Government Reform and Oversight, Subcommittee on Civil Service, *Government Shutdown I: What's Essential?*, hearings, 104th Cong., 1st sess., December 6 and 14, 1995 (Washington, DC: GPO, 1997), pp. 115-117.

[136] Peter Behr, "Contractors Face Mounting Costs from Government Shutdowns," *Washington Post*, January 23, 1996, p. C1; U.S. Congress, House Committee on Government Reform and Oversight, Subcommittee on Civil Service, *Government Shutdown I: What's Essential?*, hearings, 104th Cong., 1st sess., December 6 and 14, 1995 (Washington, DC: GPO, 1997), p. 270, at http://www.gpo.gov/fdsys/pkg/CHRG-104hhrg23275/pdf/CHRG-104hhrg23275.pdf; and Peter Behr, "Latest Federal Shutdown Hits Contractors Hard," *Washington Post*, December 22, 1995, p. D1.

[137] See U.S. Congress, House Committee on Government Reform and Oversight, Subcommittee on Civil Service, *Government Shutdown I: What's Essential?*, hearings, 104th Cong., 1st sess., December 6 and 14, 1995 (Washington, DC: GPO, 1997), pp. 266-270 (two-page letter dated February 5, 1996, and three-page list of effects dated January 19, 1996); pp. 272 and 274 (list of agencies and estimates of employees to be excepted or not excepted as of November 15, 1995, apparently corresponding to the first shutdown); and p. 273 (list of agencies and estimates of employees to be excepted or not excepted, in a document dated February 2, 1996, and apparently corresponding to the second shutdown), at http://www.gpo.gov/fdsys/pkg/CHRG-104hhrg23275/pdf/CHRG-104hhrg23275.pdf. The list provided on pages 272 and 274 includes agencies that already had received full-year appropriations and therefore may not represent a full accounting of actual furloughs that occurred during the first FY1996 shutdown.

[138] This paragraph was prepared by Barry J. McMillion, Analyst on the Federal Judiciary (bmcmillion@crs.loc.gov, 7-6025); Denis Steven Rutkus, formerly a Specialist on the Federal Judiciary at CRS; and Lorraine H. Tong, formerly an Analyst in American National Government at CRS.

[139] See "An Inside Look at the Shutdown," *The Third Branch: Newsletter of the Federal Courts*, Washington, DC, December 1995, at http://www.uscourts.gov/News/TheThirdBranch/95-12-01/An_Inside_Look_At_the_Shutdown.aspx; also, "Active, Long, and Contentious First Session of Congress Closes," *The Third Branch*, Washington, DC, February 1996, at http://www.uscourts.gov/News/TheThirdBranch/96-02-01/Active_Long_and_Contentious_First_Session_of_Congress_Closes.aspx.

---

function of hearing and deciding cases.[140] Internal judiciary guidelines, according to the official publication of the U.S. courts, recognized the "unique function of the Judiciary" and anticipated that all activities "essential to maintain and support the exercise of the judicial power of the United States during a funding lapse" would continue.[141] The funding lapse, however, did affect some court functions, with some judges entertaining motions for continuances in civil cases and at least one district court announcing it would not start any new civil jury trials. An appellate court, it also was reported, had to reschedule several arguments because government lawyers were unable to attend. During the November 1995 government shutdown, lack of funding resulted in furloughs of most of the staff of the federal judiciary's two support agencies, the Federal Judicial Center and the Administrative Office of the U.S. Courts.[142] During the second shutdown, prior to the judiciary's decision to use fee revenues and carryover funds to continue essential functions, some courts did furlough personnel "on a limited basis."[143]

The FY2014 Shutdown

The FY2014 funding gap and corresponding shutdown occurred for all 12 regular appropriations bills.[144] Consequently, the shutdown's effects were extensive for federal government operations.[145]

News media reported extensively on how the 16-full-day shutdown affected operations of programs and agencies in the executive branch. At first, many media accounts drew primarily from the shutdown plans that agencies and OMB posted online.[146] As the shutdown continued, national and local outlets typically focused on specific agencies, programs, or experiences of citizens or stakeholders who said they were affected.[147] Agencies themselves often did not report information about the ongoing impact of the shutdown during the 16-day period, however, due to the furlough of relevant staff and non-updating of their websites.[148]

---

[140] The judiciary uses these non-annually appropriated funds to supplement its appropriations requirement. The majority of these non-annually appropriated funds are from fee collections, primarily from court filing fees. These monies are used to cover expenses within the Salaries and Expenses account. In some instances, the judiciary also has funds which may carry forward from one year to the next. These funds are considered "unencumbered," because they result from savings from the judiciary's financial plan in areas where budgeted costs did not materialize. According to the judiciary's budget submission to Congress, such savings are usually not under its control (e.g., the judiciary has no control over the confirmation rate of Article III judges and must make its best estimate on the needed funds to budget for judgeships, new rent costs, and technology funding for certain programs).

[141] "An Inside Look at the Shutdown," *The Third Branch*, Washington, DC, December 1995, at http://www.uscourts.gov/News/TheThirdBranch/95-12-01/An_Inside_Look_At_the_Shutdown.aspx.

[142] Ibid.

[143] Background information provided to CRS on April 7, 2011, by staff of Administrative Office of the U.S. Courts.

[144] For more information, see CRS Report RS20348, *Federal Funding Gaps: A Brief Overview*, by Jessica Tollestrup; and CRS Report R43338, *Congressional Action on FY2014 Appropriations Measures*, by Jessica Tollestrup.

[145] As discussed earlier in **Box 4**, the shutdown's effects eventually were mitigated to some extent for personnel and contractors of the armed forces by the enactment of a narrow CR (P.L. 113-39).

[146] Websites became a prominent means of collecting and pointing to information. See, for example, at *WashingtonPost.com*, "Impact of a Government Shutdown," at http://www.washingtonpost.com/wp-srv/special/politics/2013-shutdown-federal-department-impact/; and "Government Shutdown: What's Open, What's Closed," at http://www.washingtonpost.com/wp-srv/special/politics/whats-open-whats-closed/.

[147] For example, see Stacy Cowley, "Ripples from the Shutdown," *New York Times*, October 10, 2013, p. B1; and Steve Lipsher, "Estes Park Takes Another Hit, This Time from Washington," *Denver Post*, October 7, 2013, p. A11.

[148] See, for example, U.S. Attorney's Office, District of Arizona, "United States Attorney Identifies Operational Limitations During Government Shutdown," press release, October 3, 2013, http://www.justice.gov/usao/az/ (continued...)

After the FY2014 shutdown, some Members of Congress requested assessments of its effects.[149] Three weeks after the shutdown concluded, OMB posted on its website a 27-page report compiling the "impacts and costs" of the FY2014 shutdown.[150] The publication's level of detail stood in marked contrast with the document that OMB produced after the two shutdowns of FY1996, when, as described earlier, OMB generated a three-page paper compiling "illustrations" of the impacts of the two shutdowns.[151] OMB's FY2014 report discussed the impact of the shutdown through five sometimes-overlapping perspectives, in separate sections. The bullets below provide an illustrative sampling of the contents in each section.

- **Costs to the Economy.**[152] According to OMB, these costs included overall macroeconomic effects (the subject of another CRS report)[153] and several kinds of "economic disruption" due to cessation of "government activities the private sector relies on." In the latter category, OMB cited among other things a halt to several kinds of permitting, reviews, and licensing (e.g., 200 applications for a permit to drill for energy resources); suspension of Internal Revenue Service (IRS) income verification used by financial institutions to help determine credit-worthiness of prospective borrowers; a halt to hundreds of federal loans to small businesses; and disrupted tourism and travel by closing national parks.

- **Federal Employee Furloughs.**[154] OMB cited payroll costs for "work not performed" by furloughed federal employees as the "largest direct cost" of the FY2014 shutdown.[155] As one way to quantify the furloughs, OMB said that executive branch employees were furloughed for a total of "roughly 6.6 million" employee work days, with "furloughs affecting workers at the vast majority of agencies."[156] An accompanying table broke out this total by executive branch agency, listing 1,600,000 employee furlough days at DOD, 985,000 days at the

---

(...continued)

press_releases/2013/PR_10032013_Shutdown.html; and Van Smith, "Shutdown Shuts Down 'Routine Press Inquiries,' but Not Criminal Prosecutions," *Baltimore City Paper*, October 1, 2013, at http://blogs.citypaper.com/index.php/the-news-hole/shutdown-shuts-down-routine-press-inquiries-but-not-criminal-prosecutions/.

[149] See, for example, Letter from Senator Barbara A. Mikulski, Chairwoman, Senate Committee on Appropriations, to Sylvia Mathews Burwell, OMB Director, October 23, 2013, at http://www.appropriations.senate.gov/news/chairwoman-mikulskis-letter-omb-director-burwell-requesting-shutdown-report.

[150] For a summary blog posting, see OMB, "Impacts and Costs of the October 2013 Federal Government Shutdown," November 7, 2013, at http://www.whitehouse.gov/blog/2013/11/07/impacts-and-costs-government-shutdown. For the more detailed underlying report, see OMB, *Impacts and Costs of the October 2013 Federal Government Shutdown*, November 2013, at http://www.whitehouse.gov/sites/default/files/omb/reports/impacts-and-costs-of-october-2013-federal-government-shutdown-report.pdf.

[151] The FY1996 document's accompanying letter said the three-page compilation contained "illustrations of the impacts of the shutdown[s], but does not represent a comprehensive audit of all effects of the shutdown[s]." See Letter from John A. Koskinen, OMB Deputy Director for Management, to Honorable John L. Mica, Chairman, Subcommittee on Civil Service, House Committee on Government Reform and Oversight, February 5, 1996, p. 2, in U.S. Congress, House Committee on Government Reform and Oversight, Subcommittee on Civil Service, *Government Shutdown I: What's Essential?*, hearings, 104th Cong., 1st sess., December 6 and 14, 1995 (Washington, DC: GPO, 1997), p. 267, at http://www.gpo.gov/fdsys/pkg/CHRG-104hhrg23275/pdf/CHRG-104hhrg23275.pdf.

[152] OMB, *Impacts and Costs of the October 2013 Federal Government Shutdown*, November 2013, pp. 2-4, 8-12.

[153] CRS Report R43292, *The FY2014 Government Shutdown: Economic Effects*, by Marc Labonte.

[154] OMB, *Impacts and Costs of the October 2013 Federal Government Shutdown*, November 2013, pp. 4, 13-14, 26-27.

[155] As noted earlier, the topic of costs of a shutdown is discussed in the next section of this report.

[156] Ibid., p. 27 ("roughly 6.6 million") and p. 13 (other quoted text). The 6.6 million total included furloughs only in the executive branch (conversation with OMB official, January 3, 2014).

Treasury Department, and a further 4,055,000 days at 33 additional agencies.[157] If these day-based figures were translated into an annual, work-year equivalent, it could be said that the furloughs amounted to over 25,000 employee work years.[158] OMB characterized the impact of the furloughs qualitatively, saying

> "[e]mployees not on the job could not conduct food, product, and workplace safety inspections; prepare for flu season or monitor other public health issues; process tax refunds or respond to taxpayer questions; or provide numerous other services important to the general public and the economy."[159]

- **Impacts on Programs and Services.**[160] In another section of the report, OMB identified shutdown impacts on multiple government programs and services. OMB described the impacts of the shutdown, often in quantitative terms, with 29 bullets that focused on separate policy and programmatic areas. The bullets were grouped in six categories: (1) direct services for veterans, seniors, and other "vulnerable" groups; (2) public health and research; (3) product safety and environmental protection; (4) worker rights and safety; (5) international trade and relations; and (6) other government services. In the sixth category, for example, one bullet said the shutdown suspended the issuance of Social Security cards and, in addition, closed down the E-Verify system for employers to check prospective employees' immigration status.[161]

- **Other Direct Budgetary Costs.**[162] Apart from the costs of employee furloughs (discussed in the next section of this CRS report), OMB identified "other direct budgetary costs" that executive branch agencies incurred. These costs included a variety of topics, such as lower revenues (e.g., $7 million in user fees and other revenue not being collected for the National Park Service); a halt to "program integrity" activities (e.g., activities intended to identify noncompliance with tax laws, collect unpaid taxes, and thereby help incentivize voluntary compliance, which OMB characterized as collecting $1 billion per week); interest due on late federal payments; increased costs on federal contracts due to over 10,000 stop work orders; and shutdown-related costs, such as the cost of employee and contractor time that was used to undertake pervasive shutdown-related activities—such as planning, implementation, and re-start activities—that diverted from mission-related work that otherwise would have been performed in the absence of a shutdown.

---

[157] If the figures in OMB's table are summed, they amount to 6,640,000 furlough days. OMB, *Impacts and Costs of the October 2013 Federal Government Shutdown*, November 2013, pp. 26-27. It is unclear if the "roughly 6.6 million" total (p. 27) includes furloughs at agencies in addition to the 35 agencies listed in OMB's table.

[158] On an annual basis, OMB calculates the number of employees' compensable days and hours for the current and forthcoming fiscal years, in order for agencies to use a common methodology in calculating full-time equivalent (FTE) staffing for a given fiscal year. In FY2014, OMB said employees would work 261 compensable days (see OMB, *Circular No. A-11: Preparation, Submission, and Execution of the Budget*, July 2013, Section 85, pp. 2-3). If the OMB accounting of 6,640,000 employee furlough days (from OMB's FY2014 shutdown report) were divided by 261 compensable days per employee per year (from OMB's annual guidance on compensable days), the quotient equals 25,440.6 employee work years.

[159] OMB, *Impacts and Costs of the October 2013 Federal Government Shutdown*, November 2013, p. 4.

[160] Ibid., pp. 4-5, 15-21.

[161] Ibid., p. 21.

[162] Ibid., pp. 6-7, 22-23.

- **Impacts on the Federal Workforce.**[163] In a final section of the report, OMB discussed impacts of the shutdown on the federal workforce apart from those discussed elsewhere. These included federal employees not receiving their full pay during the shutdown (including many employees who legally were required to work) and potential adverse impacts on recruitment and retention of federal employees and contractor personnel.

The FY2014 shutdown also affected many federal grant programs that provide funding for state and local governments.[164] State and local governments rely upon federal aid to fund projects and provide services that benefit communities and individuals. During the shutdown, agency contingency plans stated that several grant-related activities would be disrupted. These activities included executing grant agreements, processing payments to grantees, and investigating waste, fraud, and abuse.

In the judicial branch, as during the FY1996 government shutdowns, courts generally operated with limited disruption to their personnel.[165] According to internal guidance, the judiciary was prepared to keep the federal courts operating for about two weeks by using non-annually appropriated funds (as it did during the 1995-1996 government shutdowns).[166] In practice, the judicial branch was able to operate on non-annually appropriated funds for the entirety of the FY2014 shutdown.[167] Had that funding been exhausted, the judiciary would have continued operating under the terms of the Antideficiency Act.[168]

The funding lapse, however, did affect some court functions. Some civil cases were postponed, in part due to continuance requests from the Department of Justice. Many courts also operated on condensed criminal calendars and reduced building maintenance.[169] The judiciary also advised judges and court unit executives, in the event of a funding lapse, to post information on their individual court websites about what operations would continue during and after the initial two-week period.[170]

---

[163] OMB, *Impacts and Costs of the October 2013 Federal Government Shutdown*, November 2013, pp. 7, 24-25.

[164] CRS analysis of federal agency contingency plans implemented during the FY2014 federal government shutdown. For discussion of the potential effects of a federal government shutdown, see CRS Report R43467, *Federal Aid to State and Local Governments: Select Issues Raised by a Federal Government Shutdown*, by Natalie Keegan.

[165] This discussion of judiciary operations was prepared by Matthew E. Glassman, Analyst on the Congress (mglassman@crs.loc.gov, 7-3467); Barry J. McMillion, Analyst on the Federal Judiciary (bmcmillion@crs.loc.gov, 7-6025; and Brian T. Yeh, Legislative Attorney (byeh@crs.loc.gov, 7-5182). For additional information related to the judiciary's contingency planning for a government shutdown during FY2014, see CRS Congressional Distribution Memorandum, *Government Shutdown: Possible Effects on Federal Judiciary Operations*, by Barry J. McMillion and Matthew E. Glassman, September 24, 2013 (available upon request from Barry J. McMillion at bmcmillion@crs.loc.gov).

[166] See U.S. Administrative Office of the U.S. Courts, *Status of Judiciary Funding and Guidance for Judiciary Operations During a Lapse in Appropriations*, September 24, 2013.

[167] See "Update: Judiciary to Operate Through October 18, 2013," *The Third Branch: Newsletter of the Federal Courts*, Washington, DC, December 1995, at http://news.uscourts.gov/update-judiciary-operate-through-october-18-2013.

[168] Ibid.

[169] See "Shutdown, Holdup for the Courts," *The Third Branch: Newsletter of the Federal Courts*, Washington, DC, October 2013, at http://news.uscourts.gov/shutdown-holdup-courts; "For Federal Courts, Shutdown Caused Broad Disruptions," *The Third Branch: Newsletter of the Federal Courts*, Washington, DC, October 2013, at http://news.uscourts.gov/federal-courts-shutdown-caused-broad-disruptions.

[170] Background information provided to CRS on October 10, 2013, by staff of Administrative Office of the U.S. Courts.

Across the legislative branch, the impact of the FY2014 shutdown varied.[171] At the outset, the House of Representatives and some legislative branch agencies publicly released official guidance or operational plans.[172] Guidance or plans may vary for any future shutdown, however.

Potential Costs Associated with a Shutdown

There are many potential approaches to assessing the costs of an event, because the concept of "cost" may be defined in multiple ways. (See **Box 5** for discussion of potential perspectives on the term.) As a result, it typically is not possible to arrive at a single cost figure or definition that will be of primary interest to all stakeholders. The case of government shutdowns arguably is no exception. An additional complication frequently arises when assessing costs, due to a lack of relevant or readily available data. Nevertheless, in the aftermath of past shutdowns, some efforts have been undertaken to ascertain what the costs of the shutdowns were.

After a one-day shutdown in late November 1981,[173] Senator Alan Cranston asked GAO on a quick-turnaround basis to ascertain the costs of paying employees who had been furloughed, as well as "other costs directly or indirectly related to the shutdown."[174] In response to the inquiry, GAO interviewed agency officials and developed a uniform set of questions for agencies. GAO responded to the Senator's inquiry two weeks later, saying "[d]ata on the number of employees furloughed and the costs of implementing a shutdown are neither readily available nor easily obtainable." The agencies' abilities to respond varied considerably, leading GAO to portray limited information in a tabular format. Because agencies took multiple approaches to define what constituted costs, GAO also cautioned against comparing the extent of costs across agencies, concluding "[w]e would not suggest that the figures are any more than indicative of the *types* of costs incurred" (emphasis added).[175]

Box 5. What Constitutes a Shutdown-Related "Cost"?

Efforts to ascertain the costs of a shutdown may encounter difficulties, in part because there are multiple potential definitions of the term "cost." In addition, usually it is necessary to make methodological choices when estimating costs. Different choices, however, may change a cost estimate substantially or drastically. Consequently, there is not

---

[171] This paragraph was prepared by Ida A. Brudnick, Specialist on the Congress (ibrudnick@crs.loc.gov, 7-6460).

[172] For example, U.S. Congress, House, First Annual Report on the Activities of the Committee on House Administration During the One Hundred Thirteenth Congress Together with Minority Views, 113th Cong., 1st sess., H.Rept. 113-312 (Washington, DC: GPO, 2014), p. 13; and, the Committee on House Administration, "Operations During a Lapse in Appropriations, Guidance Issued by the Committee on House Administration," September 2013, at http://cha.house.gov/sites/republicans.cha.house.gov/files/documents/CHA%20Guidance%20113th.pdf; U.S. Library of Congress, News from the Library of Congress, October 1, 2013 (REVISED October 3, 2013) Federal Government Shutdown, at http://www.loc.gov/today/pr/2013/13-A07.html; U.S. Government Printing Office, Government Shutdown, at http://fdlp.gov/news-and-events/1768-government-shutdown-will-furlough-employees-and-halt-services, "Last Updated: October 01 2013, Published: September 30 2013"; U.S. Congressional Budget Office, CBO's Plans in the Event of a Government Shutdown, September 30, 2013, at http://www.cbo.gov/publication/44635; and GAO, banners posted on http://www.gao.gov/ and http://www.gao.gov/legal/, accessed October 10, 2013.

[173] A funding gap occurred over a weekend, with funding expiring at the end of the day on Friday, November 20, 1981, and funding resuming on Monday, November 23, 1981. However, the funding did not resume on Monday in time to avoid a shutdown during working hours on Monday, including furloughs. See CRS Congressional Distribution Memorandum, *The Historical Policy Context for the FY1997-FY1996 Funding Gaps: Excerpts from Government and Media Sources*, October 7, 2013, coordinated by Jessica Tollestrup and Jared Nagel (available from CRS on request).

[174] GAO, *Cost to the Government of the Recent Partial Shutdown of Government Offices*, PAD-82-24, December 10, 1981, p. 1, at http://www.gao.gov/products/PAD-82-24.

[175] Ibid., Appendix I, p. 3.

---

necessarily a "best" approach to thinking about costs. When considering, requesting, or making a cost estimate, many questions and corresponding options might be considered, depending on one's information needs or policy goals.

Cost to whom? For something to count as a shutdown-related cost, must it be a cost for the federal government or part of the federal government? How should costs be handled that accrue to a state or local government (e.g., delayed grant funding), a citizen or client (e.g., lost services), a business (e.g., less tourism revenue), or society at large (e.g., reduced economic output)? What if one stakeholder's cost (e.g., a contractor's lost work and compensation) may be viewed as savings or a benefit for another stakeholder (e.g., cost savings for an agency, albeit with less work effort toward the agency mission)?

Timing of costs? Shutdown-related costs may occur in advance of a shutdown (e.g., planning), during a shutdown (e.g., lost work of furloughed employees), and after a shutdown (e.g., recovering from backlogs of work). Should only some, or all, of these perspectives count as a cost? How might one validly estimate costs that occur after a shutdown?

Calculating or aggregating costs: what concept(s) of "cost" should be used?

- *Costs easily quantified in dollar terms?* Should something count as a cost only if it incrementally increases financial costs compared to what would have happened without a shutdown? Financial costs might increase in one part of an agency's budget (e.g., increased contract costs), for example, or with respect to the federal deficit (e.g., lost user fee revenue, decreased revenue due to reduced enforcement of tax law, or increased interest on federal debt due to a rise in interest rates)? Nonfederal actors such as citizens, federal contractors, or state and local governments might incur additional financial costs in some circumstances, as well.

- *Aggregating costs across different actors?* If costs and savings are monetized and aggregated, it may become possible to assess costs of a shutdown on a net basis, across many actors. In doing so, however, might some qualitative considerations become less visible? For example, if Congress were to weigh whether to enact a narrow CR to mitigate the effects of a shutdown for limited purposes, should a hypothetical $300 cost to a federal agency's client, such as a disabled veteran, be viewed as less costly than a hypothetical $30,000 cost to a large contractor?

- *Costs less easily translated into dollar terms?* Some federal employees' mission-related work presumably is not performed during a shutdown, and the opportunity to do work that otherwise would have been performed may be lost. In that light, should the concept of "cost" extend to topics that are more difficult to quantify in dollar terms, such as those associated with impacts on government services or other programmatic effects (e.g., citizens' lost opportunities to receive a service or visit a national park)?[176]

A similar inquiry about costs and shutdown-related impacts came in the aftermath of the much-longer FY1996 shutdowns.[177] In response, OMB provided an overall cost estimate of "over $1.4 billion" for the two shutdowns.[178] According to earlier testimony from OMB after the first shutdown, a portion of shutdown-related costs corresponded to retroactive pay for furloughed employees.[179] OMB also said that significant additional costs, which then could not be

---

[176] In other words, taking one particular action "A" (e.g., shutting down an agency and furloughing employees) may cause another, alternative action "B" to be foregone as an opportunity along with action B's benefits (e.g., having employees continue to perform their agency's mission-related work). In that sense, the programmatic effects of a shutdown could be considered an opportunity cost of a shutdown, even if no one's financial costs have increased.

[177] Letter from Representative John L. Mica, Chairman, Subcommittee on Civil Service, House Committee on Government Reform and Oversight, to John A. Koskinen, OMB Deputy Director for Management, January 18, 1996, in U.S. Congress, House Committee on Government Reform and Oversight, Subcommittee on Civil Service, *Government Shutdown I: What's Essential?*, hearings, 104th Cong., 1st sess., December 6 and 14, 1995 (Washington, DC: GPO, 1997), p. 276, at http://www.gpo.gov/fdsys/pkg/CHRG-104hhrg23275/pdf/CHRG-104hhrg23275.pdf.

[178] Letter from John A. Koskinen, OMB Deputy Director for Management, to Honorable John L. Mica, Chairman, Subcommittee on Civil Service, House Committee on Government Reform and Oversight, February 5, 1996, in ibid., p. 268. Separately, President Clinton said several days earlier that total costs for the two shutdowns amounted to "a billion-and-a-half dollars." See U.S. President (Clinton), The White House, Office of the Press Secretary, "Radio Address by the President to the Nation," press release, January 20, 1996, at http://clinton6 nara.gov/1996/01/1996-01-20-presidents-weekly-radio-address-regarding-budget html.

[179] Testimony of John Koskinen, OMB Deputy Director for Management, December 6, 1995, in U.S. Congress, House Committee on Government Reform and Oversight, Subcommittee on Civil Service, *Government Shutdown I: What's* (continued...)

---

determined, arose from interest payments to third parties required under the Prompt Payment Act and, in addition, additional personnel costs to deal with backlogs of work.[180] Years later, OMB broke down the $1.4 billion figure. OMB said $430 million of the total corresponded to payroll costs from the first FY1996 shutdown (retroactive pay for furloughed employees), $630 million related to similar payroll costs for the second FY1996 shutdown, and $300 million were associated with "other" costs.[181] In this accounting, OMB did not appear to quantify costs in monetary terms corresponding to the three pages of itemized impacts on government services that it earlier had identified in its letter from 1996, such as costs accruing to small businesses that experienced delays in receiving financing from the Small Business Administration.

After the FY2014 shutdown, some Members of Congress requested assessments of its costs and impact.[182] As noted earlier, OMB released a 27-page report on the subject three weeks after the shutdown ended. The report characterized all of its contents as focusing on "costs," broken down into five categories: (1) effects on the economy,[183] (2) federal employee furloughs, (3) impacts on programs and services, (4) other budgetary costs, and (5) impacts on the federal workforce.[184] OMB did not attempt to quantify in monetary terms the items that it included in the third and fifth categories, as well as some program-specific items that it included in the first category. For the first category, however, OMB attributed $2 billion to $6 billion in lost domestic economic output to the shutdown.[185] With regard to the second category, OMB estimated that the total cost of retroactive pay due to employees furloughed during the shutdown was "roughly" $2.0 billion, with another $500 million in costs added if "total compensation costs" were calculated (i.e., including benefits).[186] OMB said the $2.0 billion total for the FY2014 shutdown exceeded the total payroll costs corresponding to the two FY1996 shutdowns, which OMB said were $1.65 billion in inflation-adjusted terms. Finally, in the fourth category, OMB estimated budgetary effects of some program- and policy-specific impacts, but OMB did not aggregate them.[187]

Effects on Mandatory Spending Programs, Generally

Programs that are funded by laws other than annual appropriations acts—for example, some entitlement programs—may, or may not, be affected by a funding gap. Specific circumstances

---

(...continued)

Essential?, hearings, 104th Cong., 1st sess., December 6 and 14, 1995 (Washington, DC: GPO, 1997), p. 226.

[180] Ibid. For more information about the Prompt Payment Act, see CRS Report R41230, *Legal Protections for Subcontractors on Federal Prime Contracts*, by Kate M. Manuel.

[181] OMB, *Impacts and Costs of the October 2013 Federal Government Shutdown*, November 2013, p. 13, footnote 10.

[182] See, for example, Letter from Senator Barbara A. Mikulski, Chairwoman, Senate Committee on Appropriations, to Sylvia Mathews Burwell, OMB Director, October 23, 2013, at http://www.appropriations.senate.gov/news/ chairwoman-mikulskis-letter-omb-director-burwell-requesting-shutdown-report.

[183] For discussion of this subject, see CRS Report R43292, *The FY2014 Government Shutdown: Economic Effects*, by Marc Labonte.

[184] In doing so, OMB approached the concept of "cost" from many of the perspectives discussed in **Box 5**. See OMB, *Impacts and Costs of the October 2013 Federal Government Shutdown*, November 2013, p. 2 ("This report examines the economic, budgetary, and programmatic costs of the government shutdown."). See the section of this CRS report titled "Illustrations of Program- or Policy-Related Effects from Past Shutdowns" for more detailed discussion of the five categories.

[185] Ibid., pp. 2, 8-9.

[186] Ibid., p. 4, 13.

[187] Ibid., pp. 6-7, 22-23.

appear to be significant. For example, although the funds needed to make payments to beneficiaries may be available automatically pursuant to permanent appropriations, the payments may be processed by employees who are paid with funds provided in annual appropriations acts. In such situations, the question arises whether a mandatory program can continue to function during a funding gap, if appropriations were not enacted to pay salaries of administering employees. As noted earlier in this report, according to the 1981 Civiletti opinion, at least some of these employees would not be subject to furlough, because authority to continue administration of a program could be inferred from Congress's direction that benefit payments continue to be made according to an entitlement formula.[188] That is, obligating funds for the salaries of these personnel would be excepted from the Antideficiency Act's restrictions during a funding gap. However, such a determination would depend upon the absence of contrary legislative history in specific circumstances.

Nevertheless, the experience of the Social Security Administration (SSA) during the FY1996 shutdowns illustrates what might happen over a period of time in these situations. The lack of funds for some employees' salaries, for example, may impinge eventually on the processing and payment of new entitlement claims. SSA's administrative history describes how 4,780 employees were allowed to be retained during the initial stages of the first shutdown.[189] The majority of these employees were "in direct service positions to ensure the continuance of benefits to currently enrolled Social Security, SSI and Black Lung beneficiaries." Avoidance of furloughs was possible, because "appropriations were available to fund the program costs of paying benefits, [which] implied authority to incur obligations for the costs necessary to administer those benefits." SSA furloughed its remaining 61,415 employees. Before long, however, SSA and OMB reconsidered. SSA had not retained staff to, among other things, respond to "telephone calls from customers needing a Social Security card to work or who needed to change the address where their check should be mailed for the following month." SSA then advised OMB that the agency would need to retain 49,715 additional employees for direct service work, including the processing of new claims for Social Security benefits. Further adjustments were made during the considerably longer second shutdown in terms of retaining employees, in response to increasing difficulties in administering the agency's entitlement programs.

Potential Issues for Congress

Quality and Specificity of Agency Planning

In December 1995, Representative John L. Mica, chairman of the Subcommittee on Civil Service of the House Committee on Government Reform and Oversight, convened a hearing that focused on the first FY1996 shutdown and potential implications for the future.[190] Among other things, then-Chairman Mica raised concerns about the shutdown's planning and execution by agencies and OMB, saying "the execution of the shutdown was, in many instances, disorganized and

---

[188] See this report's earlier discussion of the "authorized by law" exceptions to the Antideficiency Act and the 1981 Civiletti opinion, reprinted in GAO, *Funding Gaps Jeopardize Federal Government Operations*, p. 82 (footnote 7). For further discussion, see GAO, *Principles of Federal Appropriations Law*, vol. II, pp. 6-149 - 6-150.

[189] See SSA's "History of SSA 1993 - 2000," chapter 5, at http://www.ssa.gov/history/ssa/ssa2000chapter5.html.

[190] See U.S. Congress, House Committee on Government Reform and Oversight, Subcommittee on Civil Service, *Government Shutdown I: What's Essential?*, hearings, 104th Cong., 1st sess., December 6 and 14, 1995 (Washington, DC: GPO, 1997), pp. 1-3.

illogical, at best, and oftentimes chaotic experience."[191] As an example, he cited the "recall of more than 50,000 Social Security personnel [three days into the furlough], raising questions about whether they should have been furloughed in the first place."[192] In addition, then-Ranking Member James P. Moran expressed interest in clarifying the distinction between excepted and non-excepted activities and employees.

If similar issues were of current concern, Congress might consider lawmaking and oversight options related to the quality and specificity of agency shutdown planning, including the rationales for excepting employees from furlough. The shutdown plans that agencies publicly released in the wake of negotiations on FY2011 and FY2012 appropriations (April and December 2011, respectively) and in connection with the FY2014 shutdown (September-October 2013) might provide a starting point for such attention. If insight were desired into agency decision making processes, Congress might weigh whether to seek access to any OMB guidance documents that were provided to agencies but not posted on the publicly available Internet.[193]

Availability of Updated Agency Shutdown Plans

OMB's *Circular No. A-11* requires executive agencies to submit to OMB "plans for an orderly shutdown in the event of the absence of appropriations."[194] OMB has required the development and maintenance of these shutdown plans since 1980. Prior to the circular's 2011 revision, the circular broadly indicated that the plans were to be submitted to OMB when initially prepared and also when revised. With the August 2011 revision of the circular, however, OMB newly required that these plans be updated whenever there is a change in the source of funding for an agency program, or "any significant modification, expansion, or reduction in agency program activities."[195] In any case, plans are required to be updated and submitted to OMB with a minimum frequency of once every two years, starting August 1, 2015.

The April and December 2011 releases of agency shutdown plans on the Internet—on OMB's website and on agency websites—brought a new level of transparency to agency shutdown planning. However, each release occurred on the final day of funding availability before an interim CR was scheduled to expire, and in the context of negotiations where an impasse seemed to many observers to be a possibility. Before the April 2011 release, it was not clear the extent to which agency shutdown plans ever had been made publicly available or systematically shared with Congress and agency stakeholders for scrutiny and feedback. In the context of FY2014 funding, OMB began to post agencies' shutdown plans on its website on September 27, 2013, three days prior to the end of FY2013.

It remains to be seen over time whether these shutdown plans will remain a permanent fixture of federal agency and OMB websites. Similarly, it is not clear if any updated plans will be made available to Congress and the public, except at a time determined by OMB or a sitting President. If these possibilities were of interest to Congress, Congress could consider the advantages and disadvantages of the status quo versus establishing a statutory structure for how updated plans are

---

[191] Ibid., p. 2.

[192] Ibid.

[193] See the section of this report titled "Detailed Guidance to Agencies " for related discussion.

[194] OMB, *Circular No. A-11: Preparation, Submission, and Execution of the Budget*, July 2013, Section 124, p. 1.

[195] Ibid., pp. 1-2.

posted and updated. On one hand, scrutiny over agency shutdown plans may provide incentives for agencies to improve the quality of the plans, should it become necessary at some point for agencies to execute the plans. Scrutiny also may inform budget policy debates about the potential impacts of shutdowns. On the other hand, such inquiries may distract agency personnel from other duties and raise sensitive issues regarding what activities and employees should be considered to be excepted from Antideficiency Act restrictions.

Federal Grant Administration[196]

Several issues and options arise in the context of a federal government shutdown in the administration of federal grants to state and local governments. The scale of these activities is considerable. Federal outlays for grants to state and local governments were $510 billion in FY2013, leading into the early-FY2014 shutdown.[197] A federal government shutdown may cause disruption to, or may result in the cessation of, grant administration activities depending on the following factors:

- the timing and length of the federal government shutdown;

- choices made by federal, state, and local officials in anticipation of, or during, a shutdown regarding grant program administration; and

- statutory changes since the last federal government shutdown that change how a grant program is administered.[198]

In anticipation of, or during, a shutdown, Congress and federal, state, and local stakeholders make choices in administering programs. For some programs, these choices may include whether to

- cover gaps in federal grant funding with state or local funds with uncertainty of reimbursement;

- furlough grants administration personnel at all levels of government; and

- involve grants administration personnel in contingency planning.

For example, when there is a gap in federal funding for state-administered programs during a federal government shutdown, states must decide whether to fill the gap with state funding to continue program operations or to cease program activities until the federal funding is restored. This decision may be influenced by the level of uncertainty the states face regarding the reimbursement of state funds by the federal government once funding is restored. Congress might consider options for enacting legislation in advance of a shutdown to address whether states would be reimbursed for expenses that would have normally been covered by federal grant outlays but that were delayed due to a government shutdown.[199]

---

[196] This section was prepared by Natalie Keegan, Analyst in American Federalism and Emergency Management Policy (nkeegan@crs.loc.gov, 7-9569).

[197] Constant FY2009 dollars. See OMB, *Historical Tables, Budget of the U.S. Government, FY2015,* Table 12.1 Summary Comparison of Total Outlays for Grants to State and Local Governments: 1940-2019 (Washington, DC: GPO, 2014), p. 259.

[198] For additional discussion of federal grant administration issues arising from a federal government shutdown, see CRS Report R43467, *Federal Aid to State and Local Governments: Select Issues Raised by a Federal Government Shutdown,* by Natalie Keegan.

[199] For further discussion of these options, see ibid.

In addition, grant administration personnel may play a critical role in evaluating the choices that contribute to the impact of a federal government shutdown. If grant administration personnel are furloughed due to a federal government shutdown, grant program administration activities such as grant agreement execution, payment processing, and investigation of waste, fraud, and abuse, may be interrupted. If grant administration personnel are furloughed or not involved in the contingency planning, these activities may not be sufficiently addressed.[200] Congress might wish to consider the role of grant administration personnel when contemplating statutory changes that would affect grant program administration during a shutdown.

Narrow Continuing Resolutions[201]

One previous congressional response to shutdowns has been the enactment of "narrow" continuing resolutions that provide temporary budget authority for only specified programs or activities, as opposed to all of the programs and activities in one or more regular appropriations bills.[202] For example, during the second FY1996 shutdown, a narrow CR was enacted that funded benefits for veterans and certain children and families programs, and that allowed the District of Columbia government to operate.[203] More recently, the Pay Our Military Act was enacted the day before the FY2014 shutdown commenced, to provide funds for certain DOD and DHS activities.[204]

Narrow CRs have a number of potential implications in the context of a government shutdown.[205] Proponents of such CRs have argued that they are an important tool to mitigate the effects of a government shutdown by eliminating funding gaps for certain vital government activities.[206] However, others have posited that such CRs unfairly prioritize some programs over others, and that they may reduce the pressure on broader negotiations to end the shutdown.[207]

Possible National Security Implications[208]

A federal government shutdown could have possible negative security implications,[209] as some entities wishing to take actions harmful to U.S. interests may see the nation as physically and

---

[200] Ibid.

[201] This section was prepared by Jessica Tollestrup, Analyst on Congress and the Legislative Process (jtollestrup@crs.loc.gov, 7-0941).

[202] For further information on the typical scope of interim CRs with regard to covered programs or activities, see CRS Report R42647, *Continuing Resolutions: Overview of Components and Recent Practices*, by Jessica Tollestrup.

[203] P.L. 104-69 was enacted on December 22, 1996, about one week after the funding gap had commenced.

[204] P.L. 113-39. See **Box 4** of this report for further information on the act.

[205] Many of these implications are similar to those that have been identified with regard to automatic continuing resolutions. For a discussion of these, see CRS Report R41948, *Automatic Continuing Resolutions: Background and Overview of Recent Proposals*, by Jessica Tollestrup.

[206] See, for example, Niels Lesniewski, "Senators Float Proposal to Exempt Military from Shutdown," *CQ News*, September 24, 2013; Nathan Hurst, "Latest Piecemeal Spending Bill Would Reopen Highway Safety Agency," *CQ News*, October 4, 2013; David Rogers, "Different Era: Piecemeal Bills Stumble," *Politico*, October 2, 2013.

[207] See, for example, Tim Starks, "Spy Agency Funding Measure Headed to House Floor," *CQ News*, October 3, 2013; Emily Ethridge, "Lawmakers Battle Over Threats to Public Health From Government Shutdown," *CQ News*, October 4, 2013; Ann L. Kim, "House Passes Short-Term Measures to Fund FDA," *CQ News*, October 7, 2013.

[208] This section was prepared by John Rollins, Specialist in Terrorism and National Security (jrollins@crs.loc.gov, 7-5529).

politically vulnerable.[210] The Antideficiency Act is silent regarding which specific organizations would be excepted in whole or part from a government shutdown. The act's provisions and historical guidance from OMB, however, suggest that entities that perform a national security function may be allowed to continue many of their operations.[211] Historically, individuals responsible for supporting the nation's global security activities, public safety efforts, and foreign relations pursuits have been excepted from furloughs that accompany a government shutdown.[212]

The actions that are taken in anticipation of a government shutdown may lessen the negative effects of an incident of national security significance occurring during this period. How agencies and OMB prepare for a government shutdown may have short- and long-term consequences if an incident occurs during a period of reduction in government services or soon after a resumption of all government activities. Should federal government organizations traditionally not viewed as an excepted part of the security apparatus be shut down, and subsequently become needed during a crisis or emerging situation, the nation's ability to respond to an incident could be delayed. Such a situation could result in increased risk to the nation and a longer recovery time as services and support activities normally provided to non-federal entities may not be available when needed. Some security observers may offer concerns that the longer the duration of a government shutdown, the more at-risk the nation becomes as enemies of the U.S. may seek to exploit perceived vulnerabilities.

(...continued)

[209] While an incident of national security significance could entail actions undertaken by a group of individuals, response and recovery efforts associated with a catastrophic natural disaster also may be an issue of concern.

[210] For information and analysis related to possible security vulnerabilities during periods of government uncertainty, see CRS Report R42773, *2012-2013 Presidential Election Period: National Security Considerations and Options*, by John W. Rollins.

[211] For example, see OMB Memorandum, *Agency Operations in the Absence of Appropriations*, November 17, 1981. See also U.S. Department of Defense, Guidance for Continuation of Operations in the Absence of Available Appropriations, April 7, 2011, at http://www.defense.gov/home/features/2011/0411_govtshutdown/OSD_04092-11.pdf.

[212] Responsibility for overseeing the nation's security interests are shared by organizations within the intelligence, law enforcement, and national and homeland security communities. For discussion of the effect of a government shutdown on DOD-related activities, see CRS Report R41745, *Government Shutdown: Operations of the Department of Defense During a Lapse in Appropriations*, by Amy Belasco and Pat Towell.

Author Contact Information

Clinton T. Brass, Coordinator
Specialist in Government Organization and
Management
cbrass@crs.loc.gov, 7-4536

Ida A. Brudnick
Specialist on the Congress
ibrudnick@crs.loc.gov, 7-6460

Matthew E. Glassman
Analyst on the Congress
mglassman@crs.loc.gov, 7-3467

Natalie Keegan
Analyst in American Federalism and Emergency
Management Policy
nkeegan@crs.loc.gov, 7-9569

Barry J. McMillion
Analyst on the Federal Judiciary
bmcmillion@crs.loc.gov, 7-6025

John W. Rollins
Specialist in Terrorism and National Security
jrollins@crs.loc.gov, 7-5529

Jessica Tollestrup
Analyst on Congress and the Legislative Process
jtollestrup@crs.loc.gov, 7-0941

Brian T. Yeh
Legislative Attorney
byeh@crs.loc.gov, 7-5182

Acknowledgments

Multiple authors contributed to this report. Ida A. Brudnick of the Government and Finance Division and, in a previous version, R. Eric Petersen of the same division, contributed portions of this report that relate to congressional operations. Barry J. McMillion and Matthew E. Glassman of the Government and Finance Division contributed portions relating to judiciary operations, along with Denis Steven Rutkus and Lorraine H. Tong, both formerly of the Government and Finance Division. Jessica Tollestrup of the Government and Finance Division contributed portions relating to the legislative history of the FY1996 shutdowns and the topic of narrow continuing resolutions. Brian T. Yeh of the American Law Division contributed several portions relating to legal aspects of a shutdown. Natalie Keegan of the Government and Finance Division contributed portions related to grant administration and the potential effects of a shutdown on state and local governments. John Rollins of the Foreign Affairs, Defense, and Trade Division contributed portions relating to national security concerns during a shutdown period. Elli Ludwigson, formerly of the Knowledge Services Group, contributed research and writing on agency shutdown plans and resources associated with the FY2011 appropriations process. Justin Murray of the Knowledge Services Group provided research support for an earlier version of the report.

Key Policy Staff

Area of Expertise	Name	Phone	E-mail
Programmatic impact of a shutdown on a specific agency or policy area	CRS subject matter expert, as relevant	7-5700	see CRS website at http://www.crs.gov
Executive branch operations	Clinton T. Brass	7-4536	cbrass@crs.loc.gov
	Michelle D. Christensen	7-0764	mchristensen@crs.loc.gov
Congressional operations	Ida A. Brudnick	7-6460	ibrudnick@crs.loc.gov
	R. Eric Petersen	7-0643	epetersen@crs.loc.gov
Judiciary operations	Barry J. McMillion	7-6025	bmcmillion@crs.loc.gov
	Matthew E. Glassman (judicial budget)	7-3467	mglassman@crs.loc.gov

Area of Expertise	Name	Phone	E-mail
Legal issues (appropriations law)	Thomas J. Nicola	7-5004	tnicola@crs.loc.gov
	Brian T. Yeh	7-5182	byeh@crs.loc.gov
	Edward C. Liu	7-9166	eliu@crs.loc.gov
Legal issues (contract law)	Kate M. Manuel	7-4477	kmanuel@crs.loc.gov
	Erika K. Lunder	7-4538	elunder@crs.loc.gov
Funding gaps and congressional budget process	Jessica Tollestrup	7-0941	jtollestrup@crs.loc.gov
Potential effects of a shutdown on federal aid to state and local governments	Natalie Keegan	7-9569	nkeegan@crs.loc.gov
National security concerns during a shutdown period	John Rollins	7-5529	jrollins@crs.loc.gov